VERSAILLES GARDENS

SCULPTURE AND MYTHOLOGY

VERSAILLES GARDENS

SCULPTURE AND MYTHOLOGY

Text and photographs by
Jacques Girard

Preface by
Pierre Lemoine

Commentary on the plates by
Guy Kuraszewski

THE VENDOME PRESS
NEW YORK PARIS

Translated from the French by Ellen Rosenthal
Documentary section by Guy Kuraszewski, translated by Melinda Herron
English editor Michael Graham-Dixon

© 1985 by Editions d'Art Lys, Versailles

First published in 1985 in Great Britain by
Sotheby Publications Ltd.

Published in the United States of America
by the Vendome Press, 515 Madison Avenue, New York, N.Y. 10022

Distributed in the United States of America
by Rizzoli International Publications
597 Fifth Avenue, New York N.Y. 10017
Distributed in Canada by Methuen Publications

Library of Congress Cataloging in Publication Data
Girard, Jacques.
    Versailles gardens.
    Translation of : Versailles aux Couleurs du Temps.
    1. Sculpture, French. 2. Sculpture, Modern-17th-
18th centuries—France. 3. Mythology, Classical, in
art. 4. Outdoor sculpture—France—Versailles.
5. Gardens—France—Versailles. I. Title.

NB546.G5713 1984 730'.944'07404366 85-11142.

ISBN 0-86565-052-7.

Printed and bound in France.

Acknowledgments

*I would like to express my gratitude
to all those whose gracious assistance
helped me in completing this book,
particularly:*

Pierre Lemoine
*Inspecteur Général des Musées de France,
Conservateur en Chef du Musée National
de Versailles et de Trianon*

Gérald Van der Kemp
*Membre de l'Institut
Conservateur en Chef Honoraire
du Musée National de Versailles et de Trianon
Inspecteur Général Honoraire
des Musées de France*

Jean Dumont
*Inspecteur Général
des Bâtiments Civils et Palais Nationaux*

Philippe Bigot
*Architecte en Chef
Conservateur du Domaine National de Versailles et de Trianon*

*without their unfailing encouragement, kindness
and consideration, the preliminary
work on this book could never have been completed.*

*I also thank Simone Hoog
Conservateur au Musée National du Château de Versailles,
for her invaluable advice.*

*I would also like to express my appreciation
to my collaborators whose dedication helped in seeing
this book through to a successful conclusion, namely:*

Pierre Kegels
for graphic and technical coordination.

Hervé Jacques
for his map of the château gardens and the cover design.

Dominique Touzot
for his research on the Documentary section.

Jean-Claude Varga
Bernard Dupont
René-Paul Payen
*who provided their photographic skills for the Hall of Mirrors,
the ceilings of the Hercules Drawing-Room and Apollo Drawing-Room
and the Bedchambers of the King and the Queen.*

J.G.

TABLE OF CONTENTS

PREFACE	11
INTRODUCTION	15
VERSAILLES AND THE FRENCH GARDEN	19
TETRALOGIES	27
THE SEASONS	55
SPRING	57
SUMMER	71
AUTUMN	95
WINTER	111
THE ASSEMBLY OF OLYMPUS	137
THE PRESENCE OF ANTIQUITY	153
FROM WAR TO PEACE	163
ABUNDANCE	173
THE DIONYSIAN CURRENT	179
THE SUPREMACY OF APOLLO	189
IN CELEBRATION OF WATER	221
THE THEME OF CHILDHOOD	241
MAP OF THE GARDENS	259
COMMENTARY ON THE PLATES	269
LIST OF ARTISTS CITED	293
BIBLIOGRAPHY	301

PREFACE

From the earliest conception of the decorative scheme at Versailles, the gardens were given as much attention in their elaboration as the château itself. This becomes even clearer in the light of the fact that Le Nôtre had already reached the final stages of his design for the gardens when the château was scarcely more than the "house of cards" Louis XIV had known in his youth; the monumental scale of the gardens already implied inevitable future additions, and, perhaps, irreversibly cemented the destiny of Versailles itself [1].

Also, it should not be forgotten that the King, throughout his reign, displayed an untiring enthusiasm for the gardens. He continued to transform and beautify them until the final years of his life, when they reached their highest degree of perfection.

He took such pride in them that he even composed his own visitor's guide entitled, "The proper manner for showing the Versailles gardens." Even though much of it refers to parts of them no longer in existence, it does provide the essential key to understanding the thought behind their creation [1].

Every theory imaginable has been advanced as to the origins of the "French garden," which Lucien Corpechot so delightfully dubbed the "garden of intelligence." We do know, however, that these origins can be traced to Castello, near Florence, where Tribolo designed the first sculpted, formal garden for the Grand Duke of Tuscany in the mid 1500's. It had parterres, fountains and statues. From then on the garden became an indispensable counterpart for every palace, each being a harmonious reflection of the other. To be sure, the genius of Le Nôtre added a new dimension to this style of garden, but did not really modify its basic design: parterres contrasting with wide expanses of lawn, and little groves nestling in wooded areas, to be discovered unexpectedly by the casual stroller—a perfect example of the baroque aesthetic.

In further seeking the origins of this type of garden, we may travel back to the villas of antiquity, to the most celebrated: that of the Emperor Hadrian. In the grounds of his villa, in Tibur, where he was to end his days, Hadrian sought to evoke the monuments and works of art which had so impressed him during his travels throughout the empire: Canopus, the Temple of Serapis, the Erechtheum. Although Louis XIV, unlike Hadrian, never actually saw the original classical masterpieces, he did wish to have them people his gardens, and he either obtained replicas or commissioned copies from the students at the French Academy in Rome. This was how Laocöon, the Dying Gallic warrior and the Apollo Belvedere made their way to Versailles.

But this desire to rival antiquity, however important, is far from being the sole source of inspiration for the decorative scheme at Versailles.

---

[1] See the Bibliography.

Preface

The sun, chosen by the King as his personal emblem, was viewed by him as "the most powerful and striking symbol of the monarch." Apollo, therefore, became the central, guiding theme from which all the symbolism at Versailles stemmed, both in the royal apartments and in the gardens. The two are very closely linked, thematically. Indeed, the themes depicted in the ceilings painted by Le Brun and his assistants, in imitation of Pietro da Cortona's Apartment of the Planets in the Pitti Palace, are repeated in the sculptures created for the "Great Commission" of 1674, consisting of twenty-four statues and four groups representing the Seasons, the Parts of the Day, the Parts of the World, the Elements, the Types of Poetry, the Humours of Man: in short, all that is inspired and governed by the trajectory of the sun.

This iconography finds many of its sources in literature. The first and most important is obviously Ovid's *Metamorphoses*. There is also *The Dream of Poliphilous* by Francesco Colonna [2] and even the "Citta del Sole" by Fra Giovanni Campanella, who dreamt of a "solar" monarchy of which Louis XIV could easily have been the king. It should also be remembered that the *Iconologia* of Cesare Ripa was the source for the essential characteristics and symbols used in the Versailles statuary.

In addition to the first two themes, there is yet a third which, through allegories, alludes to the major events during the reign of Louis XIV. It is tempting to see the group of Latona, her children in her arms and imploring Jupiter for vengeance, as an allusion to the Fronde insurrection and an homage to the Regency of Anne of Austria. Similarly, the theme of war and peace can be seen represented all along the main axis of the château and gardens. The gate to the forecourt is flanked with groups symbolizing the victories of the King over the rest of the Empire and Spain; moving on towards the Royal Courtyard, one encounters the statues of Peace and Plenty. The Hall of Mirrors is surrounded by the War and Peace drawing rooms. This theme is again taken up by the vases at either corner of the terrace, while the Grove of the Triumphal Arch commemorates the King's victories and the concessions of the treaty of Nijmegen. It was the will of Louis XIV that the château be the setting for domestic peace as well as peace with other nations. The kingdom itself is symbolically evoked in the Water Parterre by the bronze statues of the rivers of France which actually came to replace the marble statues and groups from the "Great Commission" of 1674.

In the original plans, the latter statues were to accentuate the curves of the Water Parterre planned for the area in front of the western façade of the château. Their baroque lines no doubt blended quite harmoniously with the ornate, Italianate style of Le Vau's architecture. But it took twenty years for the "Great Commission" to be completed and by then the château's appearance had been considerably modified:

---

[2] See the Bibliography.

Preface

the second storey terrace had been removed to make room for the Hall of Mirrors and the two long north and south wings had been added to the original structure, creating a majesty hitherto unparalleled. In the new plans, the Water Parterre's simple lines, barely graced by those of the reclining "Rivers of France," subtly reflected the overpowering horizontality of Mansart's façades.

Then marble statues were placed along the hedges lining the North Parterre, but they were arranged more according to their physical appearance than their symbolic significance. The Rape of Persephone, the most beautiful of the groups, was placed at the centre of the Colonnade Grove: two others were moved to the Orangery parterre; the fourth was never executed. There was a definite departure from the strict requirements of the original iconography, giving way to purely aesthetic criteria. At this point Versailles became what it has been ever since: the largest open air sculpture museum of modern times.

After the Revolution, the statues apparently ceased to be perceived in their symbolic and allegorical light. Napoleon himself referred to them as "pretentious ornaments." Other occasional visitors were far less critical in their appreciation of these all but abandoned gardens (Chateaubriand, Alfred de Musset, Henri de Regnier) but all they were really looking for on their solitary walks was a little nostalgia or a pretext to daydream.

The book we here present is entirely devoted to the celebration of Versailles statuary. It is the result of years of patient observation of these gardens whose principal ornament is the statuary. Jacques Girard strove to analyse the many aspects of its beauty, decode its symbolism and fully understand its message. His conscientious dedication led him on endless wanderings along the same paths, season after season. His sole objective was to capture the unchanging beauty of the statuary against the constantly changing backdrop of light and colour.

These patiently collected images bring to life the legends of antiquity and their relationship to contemporary history, while imbuing them with the prestige of a renewed vision. Some of the juxtapositions may be unconventional, but they are never arbitrary; mysterious at times, always poetic, they reveal the subtle harmony of sculpted profiles, or the graceful curves of human form.

In these photographs now before us, countless themes are infinitely interwoven into a sort of musical counterpoint. Those who are fervent admirers of Versailles will appreciate the photographer's insight into the secrets of their beloved domain and the opportunity he offers them to share in its wonders.

Pierre Lemoine

Inspecteur Général des Musées de France
Conservateur en Chef du Musée National
du Château de Versailles

INTRODUCTION

The beginning of the reign of Louis XIV in France marked a rare and fertile period of human history characterized by an extraordinary blossoming of the arts. Like Florence under the Medici family, Vesailles at the end of the seventeenth century was inspired by a "drive towards artistic perfection."
Artists in all fields of creative endeavour participated in this immense cultural awakening, encouraged by a king for whom not only their work and their talents, but the resources of Nature, even time itself, seemed to be called into play.
Hardly anywhere else on earth has a creative mark of such magnitude been made, producing, in little more than a quarter of a century, a vast accumulation of artistic treasures.
The gardens of Versailles are a paean to Apollo, the god of light and art, the *"model"* Louis XIV chose to follow in his role as "Nature's Sovereign."
On the western façade of the château, mirrored in the shimmering surface of the Water Parterre, are the statues of the God of Daylight and his sister, the Goddess of Night, evoking the daily rhythm of light and dark. Keeping them company are the twelve constellations of the Zodiac, reminders of the succession of the months and the eternal cycle of the seasons. Finally, a pair of statues, beneath whose gaze these gardens lie, remind us of the intimate communion of Art and Nature before them.
The daily movement of the sun was the imaginative world of the artists who created Versailles. As old as humanity itself, the myth of the sun's passage through the heavens has lost none of its poetic ability to inspire—it has, in fact, found new expression through the photographer's lens. The style of these seventeenth century gardens bears witness to a sort of rustic religion, drawing its inspiration essentially from Greco-Roman antiquity. However, in Versailles all the deities of Olympus pledge allegiance to the supremacy of the sun.
In 1664 a festival was held in the gardens which marked the beginning of the glorious era of Versailles. This great occasion left an unforgettable impression on the guests: "...a magnificent and unique occasion, a refined, infinitely diverse allegory characterizing the age... delicate and mordant allusions to ancient forebears and to the passions of the Court," (to quote an eyewitness) were not among the least of the pleasures of this fête, which would, in the words of Voltaire, undoubtedly be "lost to posterity." The pleasures of the spirit and the splendour of the events of the festival were indeed every bit as fleeting as the water spraying from the fountains.
For all their overwhelming splendour the elements of this magnificent tableau were ephemeral creations. The changing faces of the actors—the gods of Olympus, fauns, nymphs, sylvans and dryads—seemed to appear from the mysterious valleys and forests of antiquity. The mythological overtone of these scenes was to serve as the inspiration for the permanent sculptures which would eventually grace the gardens. The landscaping, the pools and the wooded groves, along with the gold-plated lead and marble and bronze, would gradually transform the Versailles gardens into one of the greatest monuments of seventeenth century art.
These sculptures can still be seen in the gardens of Versailles today; together with their legendary sources of inspiration, they have provided the theme of this book. Anecdotal comments on the intentional positioning of these statues in the gardens

Introduction

have sometimes found their way into these pages. Thus we find facing each other Vertumnus and the longtime object of his desires, Pomona; Pan and the one he coveted, the fierce and distant Syrinx; Hercules, victor over Achelous; Galatea, charmed by the young Acis. However, the descriptions, in spite of their thematic nature, do not attempt completely to lay bare the symbolism of the statues, for to do so would be to run the risk of destroying some of the enigmatic charm which is part of any work of sculpture.

In a photographic work devoted to the gardens of Versailles, considerable emphasis was placed on the changes wrought by the seasons. The magnificent orchestration of seasonal colours and shadow are like a hymn to the beauty of these statues.

The hesitating droplets of vernal showers, the timidly emergent green of the year's first foliage, the amber transparency of April shadows: all these are in harmony with the youthful softness of Flora. Later, the reflecting pools bathed in intense light, the radiant colours of the new season, and the floral opulence of summertime are in perfect keeping with the prodigal excess of Ceres. Before the tempests of autumn shake free the leaves of summer, depositing them at the feet of Bacchus, the calm glades, surrounded by alternating rows of trees, appear to be superbly draped in golden cloth. Finally, through the mists of winter, the darkened faces of the river deities bring us to the melancholy of winter, cut by the unexpected patterns of sparkling frost on the bronze statues.

The vast collection of art left to us by the seventeenth century, even if somewhat diminished by the wear of three centuries, still continues to excite the imagination, proposing ever new areas of exploration. This book, however, also focuses on various forgotten or little-known aspects of Versailles art at the peak of its greatness; moreover, a few pages are devoted to the eighteenth century, whose pre-romantic statues can still be seen in the gardens of the Petit Trianon.

The cleaning which was done at the beginning of the present decade has, in some sense, returned the bronze statues of the Water Parterre to their state of pristine purity. A number of pages are devoted to these recently cleaned statues, though others, which show the strange results of long years of oxidation, are also included. Exposed to wind and rain and all the other vicissitudes of weather, the works made from marble have acquired an inevitable patina of grey. Affected by the constant corrosion of the air, these marble statues are subject to the inexorable deterioration which affects all matter. The passage of the centuries has left none unmarked and all these wounds of time are recorded, and sometimes cruelly emphasized, by the photographs.

Any work of sculpture incorporates a form which, with appropriate lighting in a studio or a museum, can be brought out. But the statues in the gardens of Versailles are part of their surroundings, with all the changes brought about by the seasons. The tones, brilliant or subdued, and the protean character of the backdrop provided by the seasons combine to give the richest possible expression to the photographs in this book. No intentional modifications of the true colours have been made. This collection of photographs reflects the pure, unadulterated effects of daylight: reflections of the sky, shadows, and fleeting colours subtly bringing out the latent beauty of the statues.

It represents the patient work of several years and, through pictorial confrontation or thematic rapprochement, the real succession of the seasons and the actual distances between the statues are sometimes shortened. Reference to the index will satisfy the reader's desire for information on specific historical or artistic points; but if mythic, less rigorous sentiments are the goal, then it is best to let instinct be the guide. In this case, unshackle eye and mind and follow them where they may lead, as we all once did as children in "that nascent stage of life when our knowledge was first something mysterious."

J.G.

Nymph with pearls
by ÉTIENNE LE HONGRE

VERSAILLES AND THE FRENCH GARDEN

The French garden first came into existence in the seventeenth century. Its decor, initially fashioned after Italian garden pavilions and Flemish fountains, was later to become the setting for elaborate festivities. The decorations created for these events were as astonishing and magnificent as they were ephemeral. The fondness for terraces, fountains and grottoes originated in sixteenth century Italy (Tuileries Gardens, the châteaux of Saint-Germain and Fontainebleau); the beautiful canals at Chantilly and Vaux-le-Vicomte were a departure from the moats which had previously accompanied older châteaux; the intricate flower patterns were taken from Flanders, known for its exquisite lacework.

Garden landscaping became an art which was soon to develop its own school of thought. Jacques Mollet and his son Claude studied the Italian style under du Perac, and were the first in a long line of master-gardeners. In 1652 Claude wrote his *Setting and layout for gardening*. Jacques Boyceau composed a *Treatise on Gardening according to the Reasons of nature and art*, which was published posthumously in 1638.

Water was to play a key role in French garden design. The Italians were considered masters in the field, and in about 1597 Henri IV sent for Thomas Francini (1572-1651), whose descendants for generations were to be placed in charge of the water and fountains in the royal gardens. They created grottoes at the Château of Saint-Germain, placing in them mythical, animated animals and the famous "water organs".

Grottoes were not always underground, however; one thinks of the grotto of La Samaritaine in Paris and of Marie de Medici's nymph grotto in the Luxembourg Gardens (the forerunners of the Grotto of Tethys at Versailles).

In 1613 André Le Nôtre (whose father, Jean, had succeeded Claude Mollet as Head Royal Gardener) was born into this milieu. A remarkably talented draughtsman, he studied under Simon Vouet, the First Painter to the King, and in this way met Charles Le Brun. Later, he studied under François Mansart, the architect who designed the château of Maisons-Laffitte. It was while he was studying with Mansart that Le Nôtre learned architectural technique and acquired his feeling for space and harmonious proportions.

Ariadne sleeping
by CORNEILLE VAN CLÈVE

Bacchus
by RENÉ GRÉGOIRE

In 1637 he took over his father's responsibilities as master gardener of the Tuileries; and in 1640 he took up residence in a house in the Tuileries Gardens which is now famous for the works of art he collected there. After working for Gaston de France, the Duke of Orléans, Le Nôtre designed the grounds of Vaux-le-Vicomte for the finance minister, Fouquet, working in collaboration with Charles Le Brun. The delights of this château were the envy of the young Louis XIV.

When Le Vau built the "envelope" around Louis XIII's château at Versailles, Le Nôtre was asked to redesign the parterres and ornamental ponds and to widen the large

east-west axis. He worked with Claude Perrault and, after Le Vau's death in 1670, with Jules Hardouin Mansart, better known simply as Mansart. With his architectural skill, he redesigned the grounds with slopes, parterres and steps. Like a magician, he used his imagination to create the sumptuous and the unexpected: a spectacular display of fountains and pools intermingled with white marble and gilded metal statues. Within ten years' time, Le Nôtre had transformed the Versailles gardens into an enchanted place: the most beautiful park in the world.

During this period Charles Le Brun, having worked wonders at Fouquet's Vaux-le-Vicomte, made certain he came into good favour with Colbert, who needed to appoint an artistic adviser. Colbert, impressed by Le Brun's open mind and organizing capabilities, appointed, him to head the Royal Academy of Painting and Sculpture, created with the purpose of freeing artists from the constraints of the guild system.

From the association of these five men—Louis XIV, Colbert, Le Nôtre, Mansart and Le Brun— who were fortunate enough to have at their disposal a group of brilliant sculptors, the splendour of Versailles was at last born.

Guy KURASZEWSKI

Castor and Pollux
by ANTOINE COYSEVOX,
after a classical original

From autumn to spring

Double-faced vase handle
Janus: the guardian of portals

Versailles and the French Garden

Bronze vases in the South Parterre

Vase decorated with the Signs of the Zodiac

The vast transparent pools of the Water Parterre lined by bronze statues representing the rivers of France mirror the western façade of the château's central section. At the attic storey are twelve statues representing the months of the year; these statues flank Apollo and Diana, who announce the seasons and the hours.

TETRALOGIES

The programme of the Great Commission of 1674 called for twenty-four allegories centring on six basic themes. On the following pages the statues are arranged according to their original themes. Each theme is illustrated by four statues, based on sketches by Le Brun.
The Four Elements
The Four Parts of the Day
The Four Parts of the World
The Four Seasons
The Four Humours of Man
The Four Types of Poetry
These themes are derived from the iconology of Cesare Ripa, embodied in a theoretical treatise by him which was used as an authoritative work of reference during the 17th century and provided sculptors with a source of symbols.
Fifteen of these statues, which can be seen from the south entrance to the gardens, run along the edges of the North Parterre in two perpendicular rows.
This arrangement and orientation allows for harmonious lighting effects. Depending on the angle of the sun, certain gestures may be accentuated: the folds in a robe may appear deeper; the gaze of an eye may be suddenly suffused with life. This stresses their symbolism and expressiveness. Moreover, there are months when these lighting effects are heightened, either by lush vegetation and brightly-coloured shrubbery, or by surroundings which are barren and still.
At the edge of the Latona staircase between the two elevated pools which contain the Fountains of the Animals, the Water Parterre extends outward to the west.
Two symmetrical groups of four statues surround each of the pools. Most of them are allegories of matter and time. Nearby, lies the statue of Fire, the twenty-fourth marble poem of these Tetralogies.

Asia by LÉONARD ROGER
America by GILLES GUÉRIN

The Elements

The four elements emerged from primeval chaos; each occupied the place assigned to it by divine order. It is not surprising that the statue of Air is the most celebrated in the gardens.

Air
by ÉTIENNE LE HONGRE

Fire
by NICOLAS DOSSIER

The Elements

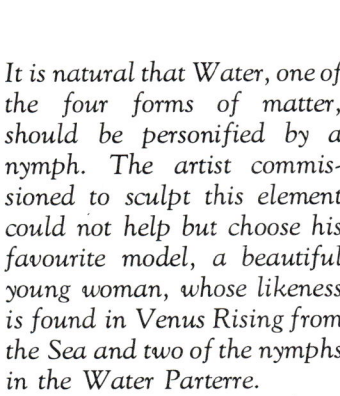

It is natural that Water, one of the four forms of matter, should be personified by a nymph. The artist commissioned to sculpt this element could not help but choose his favourite model, a beautiful young woman, whose likeness is found in Venus Rising from the Sea and two of the nymphs in the Water Parterre.
She is wearing a crown of seaweed, and her long damp hair falls over her shoulders.
Her vibrant stance suggests the flow of secret fountains hidden under moss-covered rocks.
It is not difficult to recognize Cybele in the statue of Earth. The sculptor chose to have her holding a cornucopia filled with grapes, pomegranates and other fruits. Her hair is sprinkled with flowers.
Her magnificent draped robe is much like the thick layer of vegetation and crops covering the fertile land.
"The statue of Cybele also expresses strength," and the lion at her feet is its symbol. It may also symbolize "the fertility of the earth when the sun is in the sign of LEO."

Water
by PIERRE LE GROS

Earth
by BENOÎT MASSOU

Water by PIERRE LE GROS

Earth by BENOÎT MASSOU

(left and far right)
Night
by JEAN RAON

The Hours

(above)
The Orangery garden
at twilight

The Hours

Dawn is one of the first statues to emerge from the shadows as the new day falls upon the rooftops. Her hand holds what is left of an arrow shaft, representing the light springing forth from the east.
At her feet is a rooster whose cry rends the air at the break of day. The most beautiful jewel in the evening sky, the morning star, rests upon her brow. Her face shimmers with the dew drops fallen from the veil of night as it retreats.
Noon is personified by Venus wearing a crown of roses. The erosion of time has accentuated the radiant gentleness of this statue, whose grace is more like that of a Raphael madonna than of a terrifying goddess whose lovers are her prey. At her side, Cupid is poised innocently with an arrow in his hand.
Venus symbolizes the hour when the sun is at its highest, the burning hour when it lingers and makes its way deep into the shadiest valleys.

Daybreak and Noon
by GASPARD MARSY

The Hours

The gardens are bathed in a subtle glow, and a thin opaline crescent hangs suspended over the goddess's head. Diana, sister of the sun god, leans eastward, her greyhound at her side.

Evening
by MARTIN DESJARDINS

The Seasons

Summer
by PIERRE HUTINOT

Tetralogies

There is an obvious parallel between the four ages of life and the four seasons of the year. Overlooking the parterres embroidered with brightly-coloured flowers, Ceres, portrayed as a vigorously mature young woman stroking a sheaf of ripened wheat, gives the signal for the harvest to begin in the sun-drenched fields.
The images traditionally linked with Bacchus are further accentuated when the surrounding trees are painted in warmer colours. The basket overflowing with grapes, warmed by the late season's sun, and the chalice offered to the autumn light suggest the golden vineyard, the grapes bulging with their shimmering liquor.
Despite his eternal youth, the god of the grape harvest also necessarily represents the decline of the seasons.

Autumn
by THOMAS REGNAUDIN

Winter
by FRANÇOIS GIRARDON

The Seasons

"Winter is a melancholy old man... one must see him in the cold season when the bark has been laid bare. In these stark surroundings, the large, dreary figure is right within his realm. Weariness is engraved on his knitted brow, his sad mouth and lowered gaze... he is on his way to the grave."

Spring is personified by a young beauty, Flora, a bit haughty, with roses in her hair. Her right hand clasps the folds of her robe, which an early morning breeze has blown off her shoulders. She offers her "innocent nudity" to Zephyr, her husband, son of Aurora.

In her left hand, the basket of flowers gathered at dawn in the month of May could be the offerings made to the goddess by the Sabines in the early days of Rome. As she strolls through the grassy fields and meadows, a new flower springs from the earth with every step she takes.

Spring
by PHILIPPE MAGNIER

The Parts of the World

Two-thirds of the Tetralogy statues [ru]n along the edges of the North Parterre.

[Th]e first, at the top of the Avenue of Three Fountains, is Europe. This proud, helmeted young woman is none other than the Marquise de Montespan and, according to legend, her eyes meet those of [Lo]uis XIV, himself immortalized by the Epic Poem [s]tatue at the other [en]d of the parterre.

Not far from Europe [sta]nds fiery Africa, carved in a style of powerful realism.

(opposite)
Europe
by PIERRE MAZELINE

(right)
Africa
by GEORGES SIBRAYQUE and JEAN CORNU

This nymph (left) was the daughter of Oceanus and Tethys, and the mother of Atlas and Prometheus. She gave her name to Asia, a rich land where "precious gums and spices" were to be found. Mysterious Asia holds a perfume-brazier from which emanates the scent of a fragrant Arabian ointment.

The statue of America (right) is a representational image of the stories told by navigators. She looks captivating, engaging and, with her feather headdress, untamed. Behind the flowers there lies a decapitated head which may indicate that "relations with this lovely warrior are not always free from danger."

Asia
by LÉONARD ROGER

America
by GILLES GUÉRIN

Tetralogies

Melancholy
by MICHEL DE LA PERDRIX

Phlegm
by MATHIEU LESPAGNANDELLE

The Humours of Man

As with the preceding Tetralogies, the four humours of man and the four types of poetry are based on the iconology of Cesare Ripa, who wrote a theoretical work used as an authoritative reference book in the 17th century, providing sculptors with a source of symbols.

Choler
by JACQUES HOUZEAU

Blood
by NOËL JOUVENET

Tetralogies

The Epic Poem
by JEAN DROUILLY

The Pastoral Poem
by PIERRE GRANIER

The Types of Poetry

The Lyric Poem
by JEAN-BAPTISTE TUBI

The Satirical Poem
by PHILIPPE BUYSTER

THE SEASONS

The layout of the Versailles gardens is intimately linked to the symbolism inherent in the sun's power over nature. The Fountain of Apollo is situated at a focal point of the principal lines of perspective. This is where the god of day rises from the dark ocean at dawn to light the earth.

But the sun also makes a yearly journey across the sky. As if it were shooting forth into the starry night, Apollo's chariot faces the Zodiac figures at the top level of the central part of the château, overlooking the gardens.

Just as the equinoxes and solstices mark the different parts of the year, the fountains of Flora, Ceres, Bacchus and Saturn, situated at equal distances from Apollo's trajectory, symbolize Spring, Summer, Autumn and Winter, respectively.

Three centuries ago, hedgerows and trellises marked the boundaries of lanes and groves. The sculptured ornamentation surrounded by these light structures and foliage was more visible then than it is today.

In the early days of the gardens, with their atmosphere of never-ending festivity, the changes brought about by the seasons were probably less noticeable.

The trees eventually grew too tall and were cut down at the end of the 18th century. Since then, the landscape composition has been balanced in a different manner. Most of the areas where the groves used to be now more often look like forests, while other areas have taken on a more romantic appearance.

Antinous,
by PIERRE LE GROS
(after a classical original)

Faun term
in the North Quincunx,
by DOMENICO GUIDI

SPRING

Very few flowers appear in the Versailles gardens during the first days of spring.
The quality of the light itself is the most perceptible sign of the approaching season. Hesitant patches of light flicker among the clouds as they race across the sky.
And then, with the sudden reappearance of a seemingly forgotten spring, an intimate sweetness invades the clearings and undergrowth. Gradually, tender buds in all imaginable shades of green begin to form on the trees.
A honey-coloured light shimmers under the chestnut trees laden with white blossoms bordering the main avenues.
Although the wide parterres are still bare at this time, flowered areas do appear at the Trianon in front of the Orangery, and in the King's Garden where formerly the Royal Island pool, which was the largest pool in the gardens and alive with swans, used to be.
Here, several brightly-coloured flowerbeds with particularly luxuriant plants remind us of the botanical gardens of the past.

(left)
The King's Garden
designed by
ALEXANDRE DUFOUR

(right)
The Fountain of Flora
by JEAN-BAPTISTE TUBI

The Seasons

Galatea
by JEAN-BAPTISTE TUBI

Acis
by SIMON HURTRELLE

Spring

Galatea, indifferent to the persistent and jealous attentions of Polyphemus, only harkened to the melodious strains Acis the young shepherd played for her on his flute. Acis undoubtedly had many impersonators and rivals among the fauns in the woods; the beauty of this nymph was bound to arouse their eager desires. But no one's passion for her could equal that of the Cyclops. "It was springtime, and springtime prevailed over the universe".

Galatea and the fauns

Young faun in the North Quincunx
by DOMENICO GUIDI

The King's Garden
designed by ALEXANDRE DUFOUR
Vase in honour of Bacchus

Silenus, foster father
of Bacchus (after a Greek original)

Spring

Spring

It was formerly the custom to plant all the parterres with early spring flowers as soon as Flora's season arrived. Then, as summer came, these flowers would be replaced. And in some parts of the gardens, especially in the Trianon, these changes were made even more frequently. Today, such successive plantings would be impossible in the great parterres. But in April and May, hidden away in the little-known King's Garden, south-west of the Fountain of Winter, under the light shade of the purple beech trees and Wistaria vines, we can still find a few flowerbeds with delicate shades of white, orange, and bright blue.

Ganymede was the son of a legendary king of Troy. Jupiter, captivated by his great beauty, took the form of an eagle to capture him and "bring to the heavens an ornament of which the earth was not worthy." Ganymede became one of the signs of the zodiac. This statue most especially symbolizes the immortal spring of life and the perfection of an adolescence cherished by the gods in April, when the early morning light graces this group and the northern slope of the Parterre of Latona is alive with young leaves.

The King's Garden
designed by ALEXANDRE DUFOUR

Flora
by MARC ARCIS
and SIMON MAZIÈRE

Ganymede
by PIERRE LAVIRON
(after a classical original)

April at the Trianon
Wistaria and laburnum

The Belvedere, showing the decorations over the windows,
representing the seasons (Flora in the rectangular niche)

In front
of the Trianon Orangery

Magnificent flowerbeds planted with magnolias, azaleas and rhododendrons

The Seasons

The Gardener's House
Sun and rain on a May afternoon

Spring

A sunny May morning

SUMMER

From July to September, the sumptuous floral arrangements of the great parterres contrast richly with the austere lines of the château.
It used to be that early flowers were planted at the end of winter in the box tree compartments. Flora, standing on the attic storey, amid the stone statues that lighten the imposing volume of the château, is a reminder of this rite of spring. At the Trianon, countless earthenware pots were used for impromptu flower arrangements which could be modified within a few hours.
Today, the great parterres remain empty and bleak until June.
The warm hues of summer are first displayed in the forty-four bronze urns at the north and south, overlooking these vast areas. Flowering vines and vertical clusters intertwine, concealing the delicately designed handles.
The dark shapes of the urns are soon covered in vibrant strands of green, punctuated by touches of light pink and bright carmine.
The flowerbeds then gradually fill with an impressive range of purples, yellows, blues, pinks, oranges and reds. This abundance throughout the summer is a reminder of the abundance of Ceres; it is also reminiscent of the floral wealth so cherished by Louis XIV.

(opposite)
Fountain of Ceres
(right)
South Parterre

Summer

In the three great parterres nearest the château, the gardeners never plant the same flower varieties from one year to the next. This means that summer visitors will always find new floral compositions.
This is not the case, however, at the Trianon. Great importance is ascribed to maintaining a constant balance between the red Languedoc marble of the pilasters which punctuate the cream stone of the façade and the flowerbeds in the parterres, which reflect the same pink shades every summer, accentuated by a silver fringe of cineraria. A glimpse of the unparalleled luxury enjoyed during the stays of Louis XIV is still alive at the Trianon; in those times, the flowers were changed every day. "We fell asleep surrounded with the smell of tuberoses and woke up to the scent of jasmine."

Afternoon light
in the Parterre of Latona

The Seasons

The west wing
of the Grand Trianon

*The slanting rays on late summer afternoons accentuate the parterres which have accumulated the day's heat.
Ceres with her crown of wheat at the edge of the North Quincunx does not look the tranquil goddess she is meant to be. Her lively expression could even be that of a young peasant full of life. Her rustic smile shows the joy she feels at contemplating the fields and their promise of abundance and overflowing granaries.*

The South Parterre and South wing on a late summer afternoon

Ceres
by JEAN-BAPTISTE THÉODON

Summer

Hidden away from the large parterres, there is a secret garden, bordered by an unusual variety of trees. Its flowers and shrubs will delight anyone who happens by.
The scroll-shaped floral pattern west of the central lawn matches the motifs on the marble vase ornaments in the Green Carpet.

The King's Garden
in the afternoon light

Bronze vases in the South Parterre by CLAUDE BALLIN

Dragons, fauns, cherubs, mermaids and sphinx form the handles

Summer

The Parterre
of Latona

The Seasons

The stalks of wheat interlaced with wild flowers bending under the weight of the grains symbolize the riches of Ceres.
In the parterres, under the strong light of the summer sun, the flowerbeds brimming with their wealth of summer flowers reflect the generosity expressed by the posture of the goddess carved into the marble.

Ceres
by JEAN POULLETIER

The South Parterre

The Seasons

Above the State Apartment, on the attic storey on the northern face of the central block of the château, is the apartment which once belonged to Madame de Pompadour.
From the windows surrounded by statues honouring the water deities, it can be seen that the great stone façade of the north wing is extended by a jagged wall of trees. Their immense height harmoniously balances the massive architecture; and, at the end, one can catch a glimpse of the city. In the west, beyond the elaborate geometric patterns inlaid with flowers, and behind the thick forest, lies the sea grotto of Tethys. To the north, beyond the cool groves, hidden in the deepest shade, the Water Avenue moves down towards the sea-green empire of Neptune.

Statues on the attic storey of the central block and the North Parterre at dawn

front of the trees ining the parterre o the west and to e north stand the atues symbolizing the Poems, the Seasons, the Parts of the Day, Humours of Man the Parts of the orld. The statues n the attic storey overlooking the eastern end of the parterre are dedicated to music, poetry, architecture d the abundance fruit and flowers.

The north wing in the afternoon sun

The North Parterre and the Water Parterre

The roof of the Chapel overlooking the North wing and Parterre

The Seasons

The Orangery
Parterre

Summer

Preceding pages: View of the flower and shrubbery patterns in the South Parterre from the Queen's Apartment (left). Part of the sumptuous yet intimate décor of the Queen's apartment seen from inside the bed alcove (right). This chamber was restored to its authentic 1789 décor with the help of watercolour sketches and the actual "courtepointe" bedspread found in 1955. The "summer furnishings" are made of white satin "brocaded and embroidered with lilacs, roses and other flowers, and ribbons exquisitely interlaced with peacock feathers".

Statues on the attic storey overlooking the South Parterre

Owing to the richness and variety of its decoration, the South Parterre has always been referred to as the Flower Parterre. This tradition is perpetuated every year in early summer with the thousands of plants the gardeners lay out from July to September. The North and Latona Parterres are spread around fountains which boast all manner of water creatures cast in lead: lizards, mermaids, tritons. The flowerbeds surround broad areas of cool grass. To the south, no grass is found between the bright flowers set within shrubbery borders and the uncluttered paths bathed in the afternoon heat.

The colossal Orangery by Jules Hardouin-Mansart lies below the South Parterre. During the winter this immense stone structure houses hundreds of orange, palm and pomegranate trees. When winter is over, the gardeners arrange the trees in the parterre along the box tree compartments. Flora and Ceres then fill the parterre with bunches of flowers in bright, delicate shades. In late summer, bees eagerly gather the pollen hidden in the giant clusters of asters.

Morning at the Grand Trianon
Colonnade, upper garden and right wing

The west end of the right wing
The garden Drawing Room in late afternoon

AUTUMN

Pierre de Nolhac once wrote, "One must come to Versailles on an autumn day when the light is still bright", when Bacchus spills out his "molten rivers of gold and copper" over the foliage.
The tall, free-growing trees which carry the eye across the endless vistas give the Versailles gardens in autumn a romantic appearance probably quite different from that of the 17th century. In those days, the exuberance of nature was landscaped with care.
But when the leaves begin to carpet the bare forest floor, the statues become as visible as they probably were before, surrounded by low-lying shrubbery and trellises. The delicate golden sun, now low in the sky, subtly falls on the lead and marble statues.

(opposite)
The Avenue
of the Three Fountains
(right)
The Fountain of Bacchus

North Quincunx
Term of Liberality

South Quincunx
Term of Pomona

Beginning at the Latona half-moon, the land slopes gently downward to the Quay of the Grand Canal. At the top of this gradual incline are the North and South Quincunxes. They occupy two clearings surrounded by evenly spaced chestnut trees and a sunny circle of grass. Sixteen terms in white marble, mainly symbolizing abundance and the four seasons, are scattered throughout. Some stand in the sun while others, looking towards the north, are condemned to perpetual shade.

(above)
Paetus and Arria by FRANÇOIS LESPINGOLA

Groups at the entrance to the Green Carpet

(right)
Laocoon and his sons by JEAN-BAPTISTE TUBI

Autumn

102

Groups at the lower end of the Green Carpet

(above)
Aristaeus and Proteus by SÉBASTIEN SLODTZ
(right)
Ino and Melicertes by PIERRE GRANIER

The Fountain of Enceladus (which we will see further on glistening and surrounded by thundering jets or shrouded in snow; see pages 133 and 151), is shown here in autumn surrounded by trees standing back from a grassy bank. Enceladus was the mightiest of the Giants who attempted to scale Mount Olympus and dethrone the gods. The Giants were cast down by Jupiter and crushed under the mountain of rocks they had built themselves. Sculpted by Gaspard Marsy.

The Temple of love
in the Trianon gardens
by RICHARD MIQUE

Venus rising from the sea
by JACQUES SARRAZIN, ÉTIENNE LE HONGRE,
and PIERRE LE GROS,
in the Green Carpet

Autumn

108 The Hamlet of Marie-Antoinette and the Fishery Tower

The Belvedere in the Trianon gardens

WINTER

The tall trees beyond the sun-drenched parterres with their deep green shade, the flowerbeds in full bloom brimming with the riches of Flora and Ceres, the golden cloak spread over the groves by Bacchus— all is gone. Nothing but a pale, livid light shines over the clearings and forest floors. Squirrels and robins are not afraid to approach the occasional visitor.

At the crossroads of deserted avenues, four fountains symbolize the cycle of the sun that divides the year. Three deities personifying the months of abundance lie nonchalantly stretched across their happy islands. There are flowers braided in garlands or scattered about, golden sheaves of ripe wheat and dark bunches of grapes from an immortal harvest; meanwhile Winter, a winged old man, is stranded on nothing more than a reef strewn with shells and edged with icicles.

Saturn... that sinister god, with his insatiable appetite for time, has had his fill of the seasons of life.

Even during the darkest days of the year, the sun moves along its zodiacal path. But, paradoxically, is not Saturn the same benevolent god who brought the age of gold to man? The force of nature slumbers below the surface of this rich landscape. Life will triumph again.

Even when the gardens offer nothing more than this desolate image under the gloomy sky, Janus is already looking toward the other half of the year from the edge of the vast, empty parterres.

(left)
Saturn
by FRANÇOIS GIRARDON
(right)
Latona
by GASPARD
and BALTHAZAR MARSY

During some winters, condensation of the night's moisture would form over the centuries-old oxidation on the bronze statues in the Water Parterre. This created highly unusual and fascinating images in the pale morning light.

Will the recent cleaning and scouring operations required to prevent further damage to the metal surfaces make it impossible for this strange phenomenon, painted on by chance, to reappear in winters to come?

The Seine
by ÉTIENNE LE HONGRE

Nymph
by PHILIPPE MAGNIER

(left)
Ganymede by PIERRE LAVIRON
and the north slope of the Parterre of Latona

Winter by FRANÇOIS GIRARDON
in the North Parterre

Group of children
by PIERRE LAVIRON and PIERRE LE GROS

The Knife Grinder, or L'Arrotino
by GIOVANNI BATTISTA FOGGINI
after a Hellenistic original

The Knife-grinder stands his dismal guard at the entrance of the North Parterre. He is a character from the legend of Apollo. Marsyas, a skilled flute player, dared to challenge the god of music, and almost won. The Muses, who judged the contest, gave the victory to Apollo, who had Marsyas flayed alive in punishment for his arrogance. This sinister knife-grinder is the Scythian executioner called in to carry out the frightful sentence.

Winter

There are two elevated pools at the west end of the Water Parterre. At each of the four corners lies a bronze group sculpted by Houzeau, Van Clève or Raon representing animal combat. The dramatic poses of these powerful animals portray the desperation in the last moments of mortal combat: a lion and a wolf, a lion and a wild boar, a tiger and a bear, a bloodhound and a deer.
The sudden icing over which occurs in some winters is one of the rarest and most unusual metamorphoses to be found in the gardens.

(above)
Tiger bringing down a bear
(opposite)
Bloodhound killing a deer

The Fountain of Daybreak:
groups by JACQUES HOUZEAU

The Seasons

The Saône
by JEAN-BAPTISTE TUBI

Group of children
by FRANÇOIS LESPINGOLA and JACQUES BUIRETTE

Groups of children playing with a mirror

East group *(above)* by JEAN POULLETIER
West group *(opposite)* by PIERRE LAVIRON and PIERRE LE GROS

Winter

The advent of winter often brings a strange appearance to the landscape surrounding the Water Parterre.

Day by day, the surfaces of the pools solidify, and then a thin layer of ice will suddenly form over the marble rims and bronze groups.

It thickens within a few hours under the gray sky, which seems to possess a special ability to attract and condense the moisture in the air.

In the morning, the details of the statues are coated with a thick, transparent layer of ice. A cold opaline light falls on the icy pathways, often too rough and slippery for the occasional visitor.

At the very moment these pictures were taken, one could hear in the groves the sound of branches breaking under the weight of ice: a sudden crash immediately followed by total silence.

The next day, the temperature suddenly rose and the spell was broken.

Winter

The Seine
by ÉTIENNE LE HONGRE

Nymph with a garland of flowers
by PIERRE LE GROS

The Seasons

A snow-covered grove
The Colonnade by JULES HARDOUIN-MANSART

Winter

A circular colonnade of thirty-two columns in violet, brecciated,
slate-blue and pink Languedoc marble

Winter

Ballin, one of the goldsmiths who created the magnificent silver furniture in the Hall of Mirrors and the State Apartment, left behind many works which were lost for ever when Louis XIV ordered them melted down in 1689.
The models of the vases cast in bronze for the North and South Parterres were "treated in the same manner as the silver furnishings commissioned by His Majesty during the same period."

Bronze vases
by CLAUDE BALLIN

The area beyond the Water Parterre as far as the top of the Latona staircase forms a sort of promontory battered by the winds, drenched by the rain or sun, shrouded in fog, or covered in snow.
To the north, across from this strip of ground overlooking the gardens, is the statue of Air.

The term representing Winter in the North Quincunx does not convey the same tragic force as the famous statue by François Girardon in the North Parterre. But this old man, half bent over in the cold, emerges like a ghost from the bare trees shrouded in mist.

Air
by ÉTIENNE LE HONGRE

Winter
by PIERRE LE GROS

The bronze sculptures decorating the two elevated Fountains of the Animals make these fountains part of the Water Parterre. Groups of animals in combat decorate their rims.

Each of these fountains is surrounded by a number of marble statues and named after one of them: the north fountain is known as the "Fountain of Diana", after the statue of Diana by Martin Desjardins nearby, while the south fountain is called the "Fountain of Daybreak" after the statue by Gaspard Marsy standing next to it.

North Fountain of the Animals or Fountain of Diana

Lion killing a wild boar by CORNEILLE VAN CLÈVE and JEAN RAON

Winter

Fountain of Enceladus
by GASPARD MARSY

The Grove of the Domes where some of the most beautiful statues of Versailles can be found.

Daybreak
by PHILIPPE MAGNIER

The Apotheosis of Hercules
ceiling painted in 1736 by FRANÇOIS LEMOINE

THE ASSEMBLY OF OLYMPUS

The decor in Versailles is literally peopled with ancient deities. The "planetary" apartment Louis XIV began planning for in 1673 was to be composed of rooms devoted to Diana, Mars, Mercury, Jupiter, Saturn and Venus grouped around the Apollo room. Most of this decoration still remains in the State Apartment.

Allusions to mythological characters and pictorial accounts of the glorious deeds of antiquity are evidence of this king's love for "scholarly allegories" which were meant to glorify his own achievements and endow his reign with a legendary dimension.

The decoration of the Hercules Drawing Room is the homage paid by the 18th century to the "Great King." The themes, the materials used and the thought behind it are in keeping with the masterpieces of the previous century. The ceiling was not painted until 1736.

The different sections of this vast ceiling are separated by the soft outlines of clouds.

At the end of his triumphant path, Hercules is received at the glorious summit of Olympus while the lost souls of the damned tumble below.

Through his strength, courage and "love of virtue", the hero has overcome "the most perilous obstacles" and has been granted immortality, the supreme recompense for human striving.

The marble, lead and bronze gods which inhabit the gardens are also present in this composition.

The Assembly of Olympus

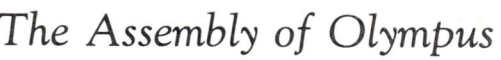

Castalia was a nymph of rare beauty. Apollo fell in love with her and turned her into a spring, flowing from a rock near the temple of Delphi. All those who drank from this spring were supposedly granted the gifts of poetry and divination. The masterpiece of Coysevox was placed in a shelter, removed from the elements. The modern marble statue, at the base of the northern slope of the Parterre of Latona, sits in the light with the same delicate posture as the original work across from the last god in the line of statues on the southern slope.

Nymph with a shell
after ANTOINE COYSEVOX

The Apollo Belvedere
by PIERRE MAZELINE after a Greek original

Jupiter, king of the gods, son of Saturn, divided up his father's dominions with his brothers. Neptune kept the seas, Pluto the underworld, and Jupiter took the heavens for himself. He only appears once in the gardens, among the terms arranged in a quarter-circle north-west of the Fountain of Apollo. Not far from the Fountain of Enceladus, he is the god of thunder who, after defeating the rebel Giants, brought tranquillity back to Olympus. He was the father of Venus, Apollo, Bacchus, Perseus, Hercules; his offspring is countless. One of his most famous metamorphoses is the eagle, whose form he took to lure and carry off Ganymede.

(opposite)
Term of Jupiter by
JEAN-JACQUES CLÉRION

(right)
Ganymede by PIERRE LAVIRON after a classical original

Mercury: the energetic, cunning, diligent messenger and tireless negotiator of celestial affairs and intrigues. This statue is sculpted with a vigour that conveys the agility of the god of travellers and merchants.

Jupiter had taken fire away from man. Prometheus, daring to commit a great sacrilege, stole flames from the sun chariot and carried them to earth. Outraged by this defiance, Jupiter ordered Vulcan to shape a woman out of clay and then endowed her with all manner of perfections.
Minerva taught her skill in the arts, Venus gave her beauty, Mercury gave her the desire to please. Then Jupiter gave her a jar containing all the evils in existence and the gods sent her to Prometheus. He suspected a plot and refused to "have her as a companion."
Mercury then took her to Epimetheus, the brother of Prometheus. He had been warned of Jupiter's gifts, but still opened the fatal jar. A multitude of hideous evils spilled themselves over the world, affecting man who, until then, had been untouched by misfortune.

(left)
Mercury
by CORNEILLE VAN CLÈVE
(opposite)
Pandora
by PIERRE LE GROS

The Assembly of Olympus

Preceding pages:
(*left*)
Bacchus
after a Greek original
(*right*)
Venus after an original
in marble
by ANTOINE COYSEVOX

The cleaning of the bronze statues near the château in the early 1980's has revealed a somewhat forgotten aspect of their beauty. In some cases one may miss the old familiar oxidized surfaces, evidence of the passage of time; but most of the bronze statues in the Water Parterre now have a dark patina and a purity which is certainly closer to their original appearance.
Bacchus, near the War Vase, and the famous Venus by Coysevox at the entrance of the North Parterre nearby, have been photographed on the preceding pages as they looked after being cleaned, with their new patina, in the spring of 1983.
In the gardens of Louis XIV, statues of Venus, Bacchus and Hercules were often replicas of classical originals. This was a decorative preference designed to emulate the pomp and circumstance surrounding the ancient Roman emperors.
Bacchus is the god of vegetation, fertility and abundance. Hercules is the man of action, always ready to stand against the forces of evil and triumph through his courage.
The most adored of all the gods was Venus, born from the foam of the sea. The statues embodying the goddess of beauty in the Versailles gardens are among the works where the 18th century sculptors were the most successful in imitating or equalling Greek art.

Hercules by NOEL JOUVENET
Venus by NICOLAS FRÉMERY

Young Faun
by SIMON HURTRELLE

The Assembly of Olympus

North Fountain of the Animals
or Fountain of Diana
Lion bringing down a wolf,
by CORNEILLE VAN CLÈVE
and JEAN RAON
Diana by MARTIN DESJARDINS

Fountain
of Enceladus
by GASPARD MARSY

Artemesia taking the poison
by ARMAND LEFÈVRE and MARTIN DESJARDINS

Heroic queens in the depths of despair: Artemesia is about to drink the cup of poison containing the ashes of her husband Mausol. Dido, the Queen of Carthage, abandoned by Aeneas, tears off her clothes and grips the sword of Aeneas, resolved to take her own life.

THE PRESENCE OF ANTIQUITY

The Olympian deities and fabulous creatures who inhabited the earth and seas of the ancient world, most often enjoying the gift of immortality, were not the only inspiration for the sculptures in the gardens.

The various realms of creation—literature, architecture and sculpture—inspired by the resurgence of the Greek and Roman civilizations during the Renaissance, produced scores of masterpieces in France during the 17th century. "In order to distinguish itself, this period needed to contemplate its own image in the mirror of Greece and Rome."

Whether seen as an inexhaustible source of legend, a moral and philosophical reference, a standard for heroism, a faithfully rendered or loosely interpreted aesthetic model, antiquity was the major source of inspiration for the sculptors of Versailles.

Dido on the wood pile
by JEAN POULLETIER

Cyparissus
by ANSELME FLAMEN

(above)
Amazon by JACQUES BUIRETTE
(right)
Achilles by PHILIBERT VIGIER

The presence of Antiquity

What echoes still remain in the minds of today's visitors of the rivalry between Lysias, a skilled legal rhetorician, and Isocrates, one of the most famous Greek orators? These masters of ancient wisdom were familiar to 17th century visitors; it was, after all, La Bruyère who translated Theophrastus. The Greek moralist is shown crushing a bouquet of poppies. He was an "enemy of sleep;" he said the most extravagant expenditure was that of time.

Term of Lysias
by JEAN DEDIEU

Term of Theophrastus
by SIMON HURTRELLE

Term of Isocrates
by PIERRE GRANIER

Apollonius was a stoic who went from Greece to Rome to become the tutor of Marcus Aurelius, the adopted son of the emperor, Antoninus Pius.

Term of Apollonius
by BARTHÉLÉMY DE MÉLO

158 Term of Circe
by LAURENT MAGNIER

Term of Plato
by JOSEPH RAYOL

Term of Ulysses
by LAURENT MAGNIER

The Presence of Antiquity

At the southern end of the Latona half-moon, the smile of Circe, daughter of the sun who knew the secrets of magic plants, is lighted only at day's end.

Across from her, at the entrance to the South Quincunx, is Plato with a flame on his brow, "symbolizing his exemplary genius." The disciple of Socrates holds his master's medallion.

To the east of the Crossroads of the Philosophers, the term of Ulysses is illuminated by the rising sun.

Mercury gave Ulysses the plant that the sculptor placed in the left hand of Homer's hero. It was to protect him from the enchantments of Circe.

The sorceress only kept Ulysses on her island for a year; she freed the hero's companions and gave them advice "for the rest of their voyage."

The marble statue of Diogenes is one of the terms in the Latona half-moon upon which the morning sun falls. The elegance with which his robe drapes over his shoulder hints at a certain concern for propriety in this Cynic philosopher; "But we are in the gardens of Louis XIV and not even Diogenes could deny it."

Term of Diogenes
by MATHIEU LESPAGNANDELLE

Face to face on the Parterre of Latona stand these representations of people taken captive by the Romans in the Danube region. With their humble realism and deep humanity, they show a little-known aspect of the Graeco-Roman artistic tradition.

The Farnese Captives or
Barbarian Prisoners
by MATHIEU LESPAGNANDELLE and ANTOINE ANDRÉ

The Presence of Antiquity

Pergamum was a prosperous city in Asia Minor where a branch of Hellenic civilization flourished. It had a brilliant school of sculpture.

In commemoration of Attalus' victory over the invading Gauls, his son Eumenes had a monumental altar built with a frieze depicting the war between the gods and the giants.

The marble group copied for the King, at the entrance of the Green Carpet, illustrates the historical events alluded to in this myth. "During the defeat of the barbarian invaders by the Greeks, rather than abandon his wife to the enemy, the Gaul preferred to kill her, with a mortal blow, and himself, with his own sword, while throwing a look of defiance at his vanquisher."

Not far from this group, at the foot of the Latona slope, lies another Gallic warrior who was for a long time thought to be a dying gladiator.

According to Pierre de Nolhac, however, this wounded Gaul and his companions in arms symbolize the ill-fated courage of our ancestors.

The Dying Gladiator
copy by MICHEL MOSNIER
after a classical original

Paetus and Arria
by FRANÇOIS LESPINGOLA

FROM WAR TO PEACE

Just as the sun exerts its dominion over all of nature, Louis XIV burned with the desire to extend the benefits of his government to other nations and combat the powers which would dare to oppose the absolute nature of his sovereignty. This was the conflict between good and evil, order and chaos; the battle between Apollo and the dragon. The forces of darkness and evil were bound to be overcome.

In paintings and statues, the artists immortalized the King bringing his enemies to their knees, like Apollo vanquishing the monster born of the deluge. This theme was developed in the drawing rooms and the gardens through a blend of history and legend. War is idealized, captives are chained in flowers. Louis XIV does not enter into hostilities for the arrogant pleasure of making war, but from a noble desire to pacify Europe, bringing happiness and abundance to the conquered peoples.

The decor of the Hall of Mirrors and the War and Peace Drawing Rooms exalts the will to bring order, the combative zeal at the beginning of his reign: "All is possible in war and in peace."

A period of abundance born of peace was to follow the conquests. But the wars of Louis XIV raised such "mountains of hatred" against France that the King's detractors referred to the triumphal arches built in his honour, not as gates "to densely populated cities, but as gates to a vast desert."

Bronze vase with Apollonian motifs

Detail from the Dragon Fountain

From War to Peace

Forming the handle of a vase at the edge of the South Parterre (page 162), the wounded serpent, languishing in his frozen prison, bites the rim of the vase, suggesting the legendary python conquered by Apollo.
Several children riding swans in the Dragon Fountain north of the gardens tease a clawed monster with webbed wings while dolphins look on. A few frightened children try to escape, but the young archer who victoriously brandishes his bow is Apollo the son of Latona.

Details of the Dragon Fountain
by TONY NOËL
Original fountain
by BALTHAZAR and GASPARD MARSY

The Hall of Mirrors, which lies between the War and Peace Drawing Rooms, was built at the same time as they were: between 1678 and 1686. The Hall contains seventeen windows overlooking the principal axis of the gardens. Parallel to them are seventeen arched mirrors which reflect the light. The ceiling painting by Charles Le Brun tells the story of the first seventeen years of the reign of Louis XIV. The brownish-red, green and white-veined marble, gilt bronze trophies and capitals, solid silver furniture, sumptuous chandeliers all combine to make the Hall of Mirrors one of the most remarkable architectural and decorative creations in the western world.

"History is taken down from the painted vaults" and engraved on the marble vases of War and Peace, which stand at the corners of the terrace in front of the central block of the château.

(left)
The War vase by ANTOINE COYSEVOX

(right)
The Peace vase by JEAN-BAPTISTE TUBI

Achelous
by SIMON MAZIÈRE
after a model by FRANÇOIS GIRARDON

Terms in the Latona half-moon

War and Peace

Preceding pages: The War vase shows Hercules in ferocious battle with the enemies of France. On the Peace Vase, the hero surrenders to the noble intentions of the King, who has given the order to lay down all arms.

The symmetrically arranged terms of Achelous and Hercules at the entrance of the Green Carpet emphasize the importance accorded to the Hercules legend in the decorative programme of Versailles.

Achelous symbolizes the primitive and tumultuous forces of nature. Hercules is the man of action whose intelligence and strength overcome the most formidable obstacles.

In the first battle between them for the favours of the fair Deianira, Achelous, son of Ocean and Earth, was overpowered. Then he took the form of an immense serpent. When vanquished again, he assumed the form of a bull. Hercules brought him down to the ground and rent a horn from his head.

Achelous then surrendered to his conqueror, who generously "left him free from any further harm."

Hercules carried away Deianira and the Naiads took the broken horn, "filled it with fruit and flowers and consecrated it to Plenty."

Hercules
by LOUIS LE COMTE

Abundance

At the end of the Green Carpet, surrounding the Fountain of Apollo, lies a half-moon of terms representing the "gods of metamorphosis." In the centre is the group of Aristaeus struggling with Proteus. Not far from there, Silenus softly murmurs bits of his deep and mysterious wisdom to the child-god in his arms.

Pomona was a wood nymph who excelled in the cultivation of fruit trees. The gods of the fields all disputed for her favours. For a long time, Vertumnus, the god who oversaw the changing seasons, longed for her. "After having sung the praises of her charms and her talents for the country life, he told her of the many fatal adventures of those like her, who had refused love, then he won her over and became her spouse."

Terms in the Apollo half-moon

Vertumnus and Pomona by ÉTIENNE LE HONGRE

ABUNDANCE

Bacchus
by JEAN RAON

Apollo occupies the predominant position within the mythological hierarchy governing the decoration of Versailles.

All inhabitants of the woods and the fields, both human beings and gods, recognize that they "belong to a world in which the sun is king."

Even Jupiter, brandishing his bolt of lightning, is placed modestly among a semi-circle of terms east of the Fountain of Apollo.

Other terms nearby also emphasize the fact that Apollo, about to move across the skies, is the source of all life. For example, Flora, personifying the rebirth of spring, and Pomona, who tried the patience of Vertumnus, surround a powerful and secretive Bacchus.

Similarly, the king set his own goal: like the sun, monarch of nature, he would achieve abundance in his kingdom through wise government.

The many rural deities near the Green Carpet are symbols of this abundance.

Many of the statues and terms in this part of the garden are allegories of the four seasons, the theme of the Fountains of the Seasons.

The statues of the Quincunx illustrate the promises of Flora, the opulence of Ceres and Bacchus, and the Saturnian rhythm of the earth.

Although somewhat hidden under the trees in the summer, they readily offer themselves to the light when autumn comes.

Abundance

The sixteen terms in the Quincunxes have a special charm which brings us back to the times when "man lived closer to the gods." They seem to have "traces of primitive theogony."
They seem to be inhabited by a secret inner life. They belong to that important part of the garden statuary which expresses the harmonious flow of the seasons within the context of idyllic nature.

South Quincunx
Terms of Pomona
and Hercules

Abundance

These statues (see also pages 176-7), reminders of this "worship of nature," seem to depict abundance not only as a gift from the gods, but as a reward for the accomplishments of both heroes and humble mankind.

Thus it was not until Hercules was able to extract from Nereus the secret of the path to the Hesperides, the daughters of Erebus and Night, that he overpowered the dragon guarding the golden apples dedicated to Venus.

And finally, the forceful "Vertumnus," which may be just another representation of Hercules, in the South Quincunx, seems to personify courage and tenacity, the only qualities favoured by Ceres and Bacchus, even in the fertile countryside.

North Quincunx
Term of Liberality

North Quincunx
Terms of Bacchus and Abundance

*Terms in the quincunxes
after* NICOLAS POUSSIN

Abundance

South Quincunx
Vertumnus

THE DIONYSIAN CURRENT

The sun, deified in the form of Apollo, is the overriding theme in the decor of Versailles. The rays from this benevolent star "bring fruit to maturity and add the finishing touches to the earth's own creations."
In addition to glorifying the sun, the statues in the gardens also sing the praises of the fecundity of nature; Bacchus occupies a privileged position among the deities paying homage to this fertility.
According to tradition, he is most often represented as the god of autumn, season of golden leaves, ripening fruit and harvests.
The fruits contain the treasure that Cybele is meant to harvest. Bacchus is the god of changing nature. He oversees the endless chain of generations "avid for life," destined to perish and be reborn again. His faithful companion, Pan, and the fauns with their "Dionysian air," are scattered here and there in the avenues and groves.

Term of a Maenad by JEAN DEDIEU and the Avenue of Summer

Bacchus by BALTHAZAR and GASPARD MARSY

Terms of Syrinx and the god Pan
in the Apollo half-moon
by SIMON MAZIÈRE

The Dionysian Current

Term of Pan
by DOMENICO GUIDI
after NICOLAS POUSSIN

Faun
by PHILIPPE BUYSTER

Young faun
by DOMENICO GUIDI
after NICOLAS POUSSIN

Bacchus
by THOMAS REGNAUDIN

Term of a maenad
after NICOLAS POUSSIN

The Dionysian Current

The Dionysian Current

These statues show the mystery of ancient times when man and nature were one. As a "God who is all-encompassing and omnipresent", Pan personifies the chaotic "impenetrable and invicible" forces of nature.
He was raised by the nymphs of Arcadia and was a companion to Bacchus. Like the fauns, he was born with horns and cloven feet. The smile of these supernatural beings reveals an intimate communion with nature, a secret joy, a hidden knowledge all their own.

"Laden with the ripened grapes of autumn, the field becomes purple, the harvest flows to the brim. What is the blessing Bacchus brings us deserving such extensive celebration?" In imitation of the marble faun to the right, the young satyr engages in the manly pleasure of squeezing grapes, extracting the essence of sun and water, feeling their plump shape between his fingers.

Term of Pan
by SIMON MAZIÈRE

Child satyr
by PIERRE LE GROS

Term of a faun with grapes
by JACQUES HOUZEAU

Ceiling of the Apollo Drawing Room
by CHARLES DE LA FOSSE

THE SUPREMACY OF APOLLO

Never has anyone, more than Louis XIV, so clearly established the striking parallel between king and sun.
"Beyond a doubt, this heavenly body represents the most vivid and beautiful image of a monarch because of its unique nature: its brilliance, the light it sheds on the planets surrounding it like courtiers, the just and impartial distribution of its light to all regions of the earth, the good it produces, creating joy and activity in all areas of life, its relentless yet calm movement and the constant and unchanging path from which it never deviates or strays."
Of all the themes to which the great artists of the time devoted their talents, that of Apollo was naturally the most important.
Thus, Charles de La Fosse, an excellent colourist and student of Lebrun, painted the centre section of the ceiling in the Apollo Drawing Room at the end of the State Apartment. The sun god, glowing with youth and surrounded by the seasons, ventures forth to light the world.
France, who can be seen wearing a robe covered in golden fleurs-de-lis, "seems to be fully at peace, owing to the constant attention paid by the King to the happiness of his subjects."
The theme of Apollo, a heritage from the 17th century, is even more important in the gardens, with their solar arrangement, than in the château itself.

190 The east side at dawn

The south side at noon

The Supremacy of Apollo

Some summer nights, Louis XIV would invite the royal court to admire the sunset from the top of the Latona steps. This is where two urns dedicated to Apollo are to be found. The handles symbolize the beginning of the sun's skyward path.

The hours move daily across the face of Apollo. The leaves surrounding his head point inward towards the god of light; there are the palm leaves under which he was born on the Island of Delos and the laurel branches immortalizing his love for the nymph Daphne.

The Sun Vase by JEAN DROUILLY
in the March light

The west side
at sunset

On the attic storey of the westernmost façade of the château, above the cornice supported by the fourteen columns of the centre block, are the statues of Apollo and Diana, flanked by the twelve signs of the zodiac. The distance between the god of day and the goddess of night is the ideal space for laying out the mythological theme of the gardens.

From the very beginning, the château was oriented in a certain direction. This channeled and reinforced the majestic, Louis XIV style in which this solar arrangement was executed.

A visitor continuing along this axis westward will come to the edge of the Latona steps and discover the main view of the gardens between the Sun Vases, whose major themes relate to the legend of Apollo. When Jupiter fell in love with the beauty of Latona, she was unable to resist the king of the gods. Soon, she could "no longer hide the consequences of her weakness" and, least of all, from Juno. In her jealousy, she banished Latona from the heavens and made the Earth swear never to offer her a resting place.

Latona was never able to find asylum in her wanderings, but Neptune took pity on her. He struck the sea bottom with his trident and created the island of Delos. It was a floating island slightly hidden under the surface of the water and this released it from the oath taken by the Earth.

It was on this island, leaning against a palm tree or holding onto an olive branch, that she gave birth to the twins, Apollo and Diana. But the queen of the gods continued to bear her jealous wrath against Latona, causing her to take flight with the two children in her arms.

The Sun Vase
by JEAN DROUILLY

The Fountain of Latona
by BALTHAZAR and GASPARD MARSY

The Insult to Latona

At the time of day when the hills and plains are baked by the burning sun, Latona, exhausted and consumed with thirst, reached the bottom of a cool valley, where she spied the glimmer of a clear, cool pond. "The thirsty children had drunk the last drop of milk from her breasts." The young mother hastened to the shore.

No sooner had she knelt to drink, than the peasants, who had been cutting reeds on the shores of the pond, began mocking her. Not only did they insult the poor woman, they also prevented her from drawing the clear water. She begged them: "Please have pity on these children I am carrying—they are holding out their little arms to you... if you give me a little water you will be saving my life." In reply, the vile creatures trampled the muddy bottom of the pond.

At this point, Latona put an end to her begging. "Her anger became stronger than her thirst... She could no longer bear speaking like anyone less than a goddess. Raising her hands to the heavens, she cried, "May you live for ever in your pond!"

Latona and her children, Apollo and Diana by BALTHAZAR MARSY

The Supremacy of Apollo

Her wish was granted. Jupiter converted "into beasts those barbarians whom the suffering beauty had been unable to conquer." Their bodies have taken the form of frogs and lizards who live on the shores of swamps, both swimming on the surface of the water, resting on the shores, and plunging among the reeds in the murky depths.

Their voices are hoarse. "Even in the water, this vulgar brood keeps trying to yell insults which ever widen their already gaping mouths."

Initially, the marble group was located in a place which was both more realistic and more appropriate to the legend faithfully depicted by the sculptors; the rock supporting it emerged directly from the water. But the final pyramidal shape dramatizes the imploring Latona whose wish was later granted by Jupiter.

Details of the Latona Fountain by BALTHAZAR and GASPARD MARSY

Preceding pages:
Apollo's chariot
by JEAN-BAPTISTE TUBI

The Grove of the Domes in Spring
Acis and Galatea
by JEAN-BAPTISTE TUBI

Walking down the Green Carpet, whose perspective is continued beyond the Apollo fountain by the Grand Canal, we come to the Grove of the Domes on the right; we saw a wintry prospect of this grove earlier (pages 134-5).

Two famous statues which had been removed in the 19th century were returned to the positions in the grove which they had originally occupied in 1684.

These two statues, sculpted in 1667 by Jean-Baptiste Tubi, were originally placed in the Grotto of Tethys, where they accompanied the group "Apollo tended by the nymphs" by François Girardon and Thomas Regnaudin and the groups of the "sun horses" by Balthazar and Gaspard Marsy and Gilles Guérin. The Grotto of Tethys is described in "The loves of Cupid and Psyche", a poem by La Fontaine.

In 1684, the rocky shelter which so harmoniously contrasted with the statues was destroyed. The statues were then taken to the Grove of the Domes.

Then in 1704, the groups of Apollo and the sun horses were moved again. Acis and Galatea were not included in this move, and remained in the grove, to which other statues were brought.

Ino, a victim of Juno's rage, threw herself into the sea. At Venus' request, she was received by Neptune and admitted to the ranks of the water deities.

In a dream, Apollo warned Arion that the sailors on his ship were plotting to do away with him. He took his lute and began to sing. The dolphins gathered around his ship; Arion then dived into the sea and was carried to the shore on the back of one of them.

The Grove of the Domes
Ino
by JOSEPH RAYOL
Arion
by JEAN RAON

The Supremacy of Apollo

The apparent path of the sun is illustrated by two of the most important works of sculpture at Versailles.

The early hours of the sun's path are represented in the centre of a "vast pool of placid water which seems to carry the ripples of the Grand Canal into the gardens."

The day begins; Apollo "has left the deep dwelling place of Tethys" and rushes forward to light the earth on his glistening chariot, pulled by four horses who "make the dew by shaking their manes."

Four tritons blowing into conch shells triumphantly announce to the world below "the awaited arrival of a new day..." The once gilded lead group "is reflected in the shimmering water which takes on all the first rays of the sun, while all around the mass of trees stand by in quiet mystery."

Since the 18th century, the dwelling place where the sun "rests" after dropping below the horizon has been a romantic grove. Tall trees surround a clearing hidden by bushes.

At the edge of a pond, sharp rocks shelter the marble group, symbolizing the prelude to the night, when, in a sea grotto unknown to humans, the god of day and the enigmatic goddess of the seas come together.

A few rough stone columns form the entrance to the shallow cave which is quite different from the "damp caverns covered with the treasures of Amphitrite" familiar to the 17th century.

Apollo tended by the nymphs by FRANÇOIS GIRARDON and THOMAS REGNAUDIN

Day is done. The horses of the sun, shimmering in the light, have just finished their ride. As they enter the cavern of Tethys, the darkness radiates. Frothing at the mouth and exhausted, they slowly quiet down in the familiar shadows which greet them every night. After unhitching them, the Tritons hurry to slake their thirst with brimming cups of godly potions and pat their burning flanks with cool caresses.

The horses of the sun
by BALTHAZAR and GASPARD MARSY

Mysterious Tethys

Nymph emerging from the back of the cavern
by THOMAS REGNAUDIN

The Supremacy of Apollo

Apollo tended by the nymphs: details of the group

Melicerte drying the feet of Apollo by FRANÇOIS GIRARDON

The Supremacy of Apollo

Apollo tended by the nymphs: details of the group

Doris pouring the ointment
by FRANÇOIS GIRARDON

The Supremacy of Apollo

"In her arms Delphine holds an ancient Greek vase,
At Apollo's side, Clymene sighs in vain:
Alas!
Apollo is oblivious to the charms of these beauties:
His heart belongs to her whom he is about to rejoin.

La Fontaine,
"The Loves of Cupid and Psyche", Book I

Two of the nymphs tending Apollo,
one holding a water pitcher, the other arranging his hair
by THOMAS REGNAUDIN

The Supremacy of Apollo

Just as the sculpted marble Apollo in the cave is a symbol of the King, so too is the triumphant gilded charioteer in the fountain. It represents an idealized image of the absolute monarch who wields his power in all areas of human activity, just as the sun extends its benevolent domination over all of nature.

Nymph in the Grotto of Tethys by FRANÇOIS GIRARDON Apollo riding his chariot at dawn by JEAN-BAPTISTE TUBI.

Rather curiously, it was not until relatively late that the King's bedchamber was installed in its obvious position, at the heart of the château. In 1661, the young Louis XIV began "governing on his own." Orientation was not of great significance to the King when planning the new additions to his father's château. The King's apartment, then facing north, was rather poorly lit.

The decor became almost symbolic in itself. The "planetary" drawing rooms surround the King's Great Bedchamber, and, at the centre of the ceiling, Apollo sets out on his chariot to light up the earth. It is the very path followed by the sun above the gardens.

In 1682, when the court and the government were moved to Versailles, the role attributed to this Apartment of the Planets or the State Apartment led Louis XIV to transfer his bedchamber in 1684 to the end of the Marble Courtyard, facing the sunrise.

But it was not until 1701 that the King's Bedchamber finally occupied a place directly in line with the overall orientation of Versailles. From then on, it was installed in the centre of the château and recognized as its focal point. This room laden with gold, but harmoniously ornate, is right where it should be with respect to the trajectory of Apollo.

During the last years of Louis XIV's reign it was in this chamber, where the daily ceremonies centred on the King's waking and retiring, that the divine right monarchy was sanctified.

In 1980, the restoration of this chamber, which took patience and more than twenty-five years of work, gave it back the splendour which had been dulled and disfigured by time and the vicissitudes of history.

The King's Bedchamber

The Supremacy of Apollo

(above and near left)
Daylight
by LAZZARO BALDI

(above and far left)
Air
by ÉTIENNE LE HONGRE

IN CELEBRATION OF WATER

As part of the immense undertaking involved in expanding the château and gardens, Louis XIV first had an ingenious water system built. It consisted of pipes, hydraulic pumps and special ponds for draining the rainwater from the plateaux and hills surrounding Versailles.

Similar to a cascade system, this water flowed from fountain to fountain, down from the higher points, to be collected at the lowest point of the gardens: the Grand Canal. François Francini and Claude Denis were responsible for calculating the height of each fountain and controlling the flow rate of the system.

As the number of fountains increased, the volume of available water gradually became insufficient. In 1681, construction of the "machine de Marly" on the Seine began: fourteen enormous wheels driving two hundred and twenty-five pumps. Then, in 1684, Vauban, the most celebrated military engineer of the time, was called in. He began construction of a colossal aqueduct which was to carry water from the Eure River to Versailles; but war broke out and this too ambitious project was never completed.

From then on, Versailles had to be content with a much smaller quantity of water. This may have been a blessing in disguise, however, because Louis XIV, in order to compensate for this and maintain the interest of visitors, began peopling the fountains and pools with sculptures, many of which are the subject of this book.

The Pyramid
by FRANÇOIS GIRARDON

The Chariot of Apollo by JEAN-BAPTISTE TUBI

Sprays in the shape of a fleur-de-lis

In Celebration of Water

Preceding pages: the Fountain of Latona and the Lizards by BALTHAZAR and GASPARD MARSY

The Bathing Nymphs of Diana by FRANÇOIS GIRARDON

In Celebration of Water

"In a cavern where spring tides flow"

Hyale, Crocale, Rhanis, Nephele, Phiale, Psecas... nymphs of Diana

228 The Rockwork Grove

The Fountain of Winter by FRANÇOIS GIRARDON

230 The Seine by ÉTIENNE LE HONGRE — The Loiret by THOMAS REGNAUDIN

In Celebration of Water

At each corner of the Water Parterre fountain is a statue of a "vigorous old man, still in the prime of his maturity" facing a woman of powerful beauty; they symbolize the rivers that flow throughout and fertilize France.
Eight water nymphs accompanying these water deities recline along the edge of the pool. Their shoulders are as smooth as stone after centuries of being tossed along by torrents of water.
The changing light falling on these statues fully emphasizes the "delight in form" which, as in Greek sculpture, characterizes the art of Versailles at its best.

Nymph
by PIERRE LE GROS

In Celebration of Water

The Garonne
by ANTOINE COYSEVOX

Nymph
by PIERRE LE GROS

The Loire
by THOMAS REGNAUDIN

In Celebration of Water

The Marne, one of the rivers in the Water Parterre, is seated on the edge of the north pool. The Saône, reclining along the rim of the south pool, embodies the fertility of Burgundy.

236 The Marne
by ÉTIENNE LE HONGRE

The Saône
by JEAN-BAPTISTE TUBI

Nymph
by ÉTIENNE LE HONGRE

The Rhône
by JEAN-BAPTISTE TUBI

THE THEME OF CHILDHOOD

"The theme of youth must be present in everything we do." These words were spoken by Louis XIV to Mansart in 1698 when the Menagerie was being altered to please the Duchess of Burgundy, whose youthful charm and spirit so delighted the sixty-year-old King. "We must have children everywhere."

It is not surprising that these phrases spoken by the aging King became legendary: they apply perfectly to all of Versailles.

Indeed, childhood is sometimes the only theme of a decor, as is the case in the Water Avenue. It can be found in the fountains, cheerfully accompanying the gods of the seasons. It is always part of the ornamentation in the groves and great flowered parterres. It is one of the essential elements in the statues in the Water Parterre. Carefree and playful, it is reflected in the farthest pools of the Trianon.

In order to satisfy the King's profound, insatiable love for this wonderful period of life when our senses awaken to the beauty of the world, the artists created countless little musicians and dancers, child-gods, young laughing satyrs, playful tritons, dreamy and mischievous angels.

Young satyr
by GASPARD MARSY

Vase depicting the childhood of Mars
by JEAN HARDY

The Rockwork Grove

Detail from a candlestand in gilded lead

The Theme of Childhood

So many of the lead statues in Versailles were sculpted with such subtle, spirited and lively contours that they almost look as if they were made of clay. The replacement of the original decor in the Water Avenue fountain, the destruction of certain groves and the scattering of certain fragile works which adorned the gardens in the 17th century unfortynately did away with a large number of lively figures of children.

However, some excellent examples still remain, such as this bas-relief in the Rockwork Grove. In the Trianon, other delightful works of childhood love can be found.

Gardens of the Trianon

Lead vase in the Hall of Classical Statues
by ROBERT LE LORRAIN

The Theme of Childhood

Throughout the months of summer, only a small amount of light is able to filter through the tall canopy of trees lining the Water Avenue.
The statues under the pink basins are constantly wreathed in shadow.

Details of the fountains in the Water Avenue Groups by ÉTIENNE LE HONGRE, PIERRE LE GROS and LOUIS LERAMBERT

The Theme of Childhood

When the fountains begin to play, the young tritons, suddenly glistening with water, come to life.
Little satyrs, musicians and dancers seem to live anew under the steamy downpour carried off by the afternoon breeze.

(above and left)
Tritons
by PIERRE LE GROS

The Water Avenue in summer

Group of children by PIERRE LE GROS

From July
to September
in the parterres
and groves

The Theme of Childhood

In the thickly-wooded northern section of the gardens, the tall trees form a canopy with only occasional clearings. In the centre of one of these clearings lies a lead-rimmed fountain. A brown rock scattered with painted flowers in natural colours rises out of the centre. The warm tones of the modern patina are not very different from the original gilded surfaces of the statues.

The Children's Island Fountain
by JEAN HARDY

Details of the bronze vases
in the South Parterre

250 Young triton and nymph with a garland of rushes

Bronze groups in the Water Parterre by PIERRE LE GROS, in the morning light

The Theme of Childhood

At each of the eight corners of the pools in the Water Parterre is a group composed exclusively of children. In addition, each of the nude figures outstretched on the rims has a cheerful little companion representing "a spirit of water, air and land."
Boys and girls play with garlands, birds, shells and reeds. Some hold mirrors, as if trying to capture the infinite reflections of the sun in the pools, from the cool, blue light of morning to the coppery tones of sunset.

Following pages: The Water Parterre under the setting sun. Groups of children by CORNEILLE VAN CLÈVE *and* JEAN POULLETIER

Boy with bird

The Theme of Childhood

254 Young triton from the Water Cabinet

The essential beauty of these bronze and lead sculptures, in addition to the inherent charm of childhood, is accentuated and dramatized by the effect of weathering.
The years have made their contribution to the charm of the statues in the gardens of Versailles.

Boy with bird in the Water Parterre by SIMON MAZIÈRE

The Theme of Childhood

Ceres and a cupid in the Fountain of Summer by THOMAS REGNAUDIN

DOCUMENTARY SECTION

The gardens at dusk:
a view across the
Water Parterre, seen
from the terrace of
the château

MAP OF THE GARDENS
and
List of the Sculptures

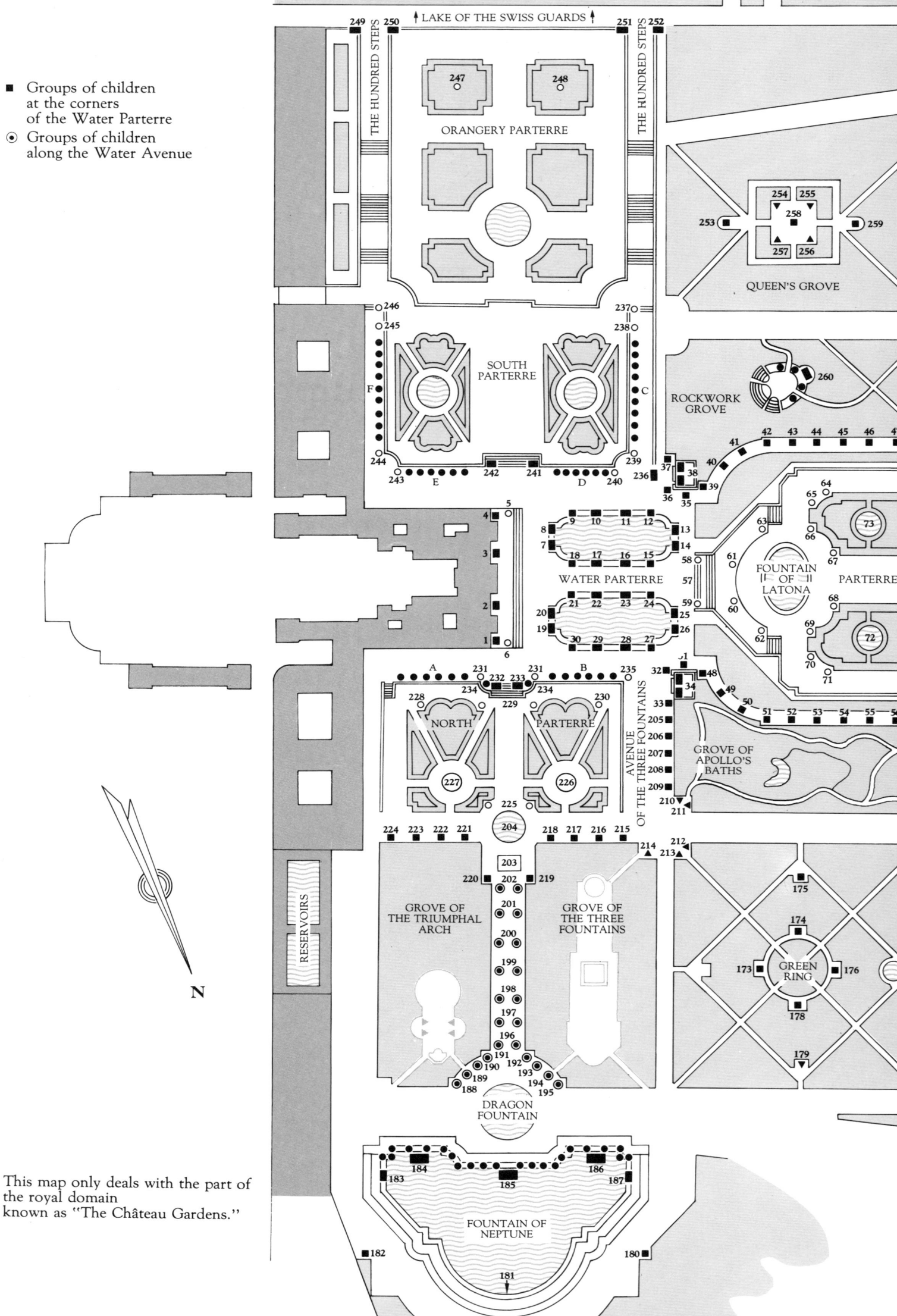

- Groups of children at the corners of the Water Parterre
- Groups of children along the Water Avenue

This map only deals with the part of the royal domain known as "The Château Gardens."

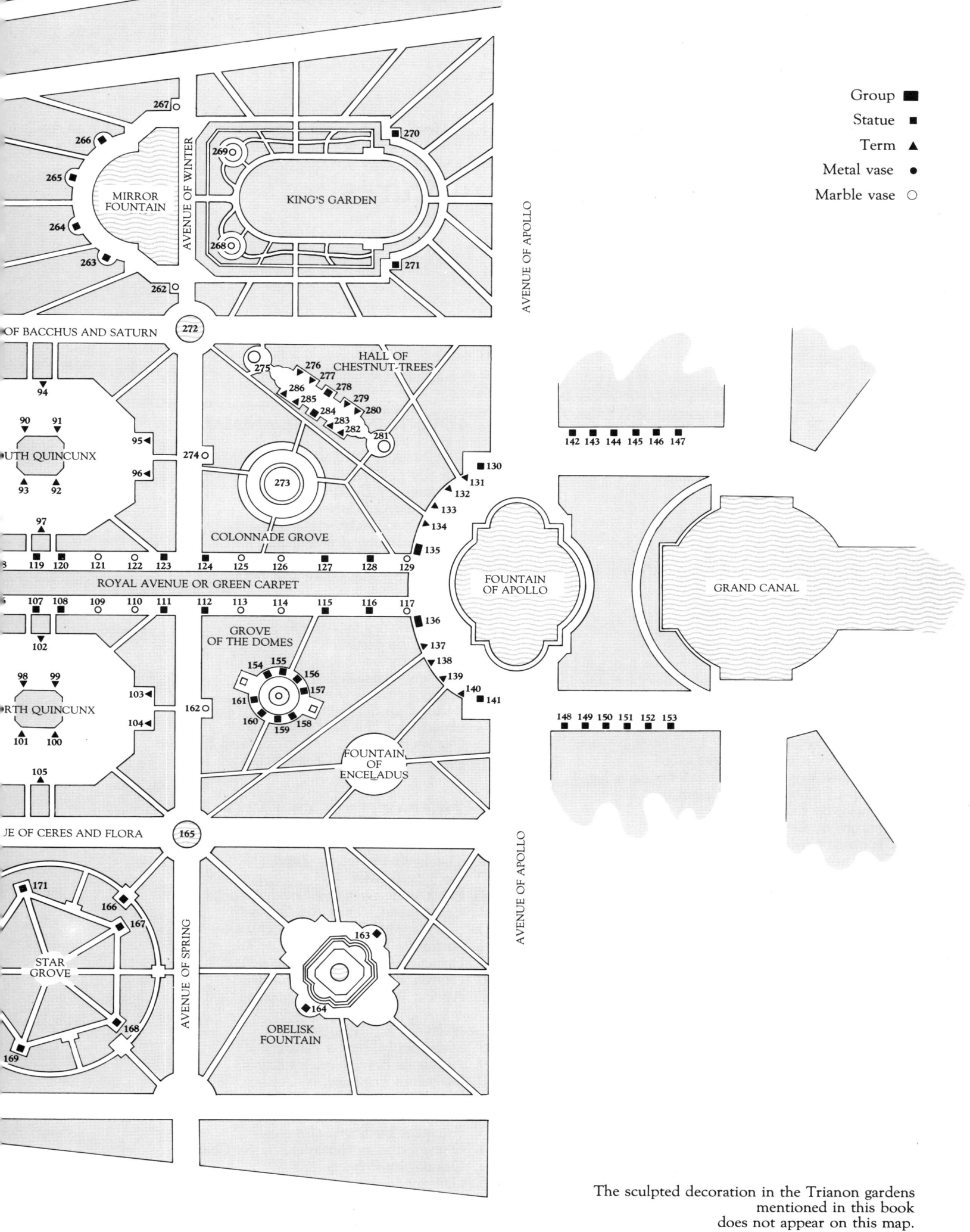

The sculpted decoration in the Trianon gardens mentioned in this book does not appear on this map.

List of the Sculptures

TERRACE

In front of the central section of the château: 4 bronze statues in the classical style
1. Bacchus at rest
2. Apollo Belvedere
3. Antinous Belvedere
4. Silenus holding Bacchus

Placed below the Peace and War Drawing Rooms respectively:
5. Peace Vase, by *Tubi*
6. War Vase, by *Coysevox*

WATER PARTERRE

SOUTH POOL
7. The Loiret River, by *Regnaudin*
8. The Loire River, by *Regnaudin*
9. Group of Children, by *Lespingola*
10. Nymph, by *Le Hongre*
11. Nymph, by *Le Hongre*
12. Group of Children, by *Mazière*
13. The Rhône River, by *Tubi*
14. The Saône River, by *Tubi*
15. Group of Children, by *Laviron* and *Le Gros*
16. Nymph, by *Raon*
17. Nymph, by *Raon*
18. Group of Children, by *Poulletier*

NORTH POOL
19. The Garonne River, by *Coysevox*
20. The Dordogne River, by *Coysevox*
21. Group of Children, by *Dugoulon*
22. Nymph, by *Le Gros*
23. Nymph, by *Le Gros*
24. Group of Children, by *Granier*
25. The Marne River, by *Le Hongre*
26. The Seine River, by *Le Hongre*
27. Group of Children, by *Buirette* and *Lespingola*
28. Nymph, by *Magnier*
29. Nymph, by *Magnier*
30. Group of Children, by *Van Clève*

FOUNTAINS OF THE ANIMALS

FOUNTAIN OF EVENING
31. Air, by *Le Hongre*
32. Evening, by *Desjardins*
33. Noon, by G. *Marsy*
34. Fighting animals:
    a lion bringing down a boar
    a lion bringing down a wolf
    bronzes by *Van Clève* and *Raon*

FOUNTAIN OF DAYBREAK
35. Daybreak, by G. *Marsy*
36. Spring, by *Magnier*
37. Water, by *Le Gros*
38. Fighting animals:
    a tiger bringing down a bear
    a bloodhound killing a stag
    bronzes by *Houzeau*
    Numbers 31, 32, 33, 35, 36 and 37 were part of the Great Commission of 1674

THE PARTERRE OF LATONA

SOUTH SLOPE
39. The Lyric Poem, by *Tubi*
40. Fire, by *Dossier*
41. Farnese captives, by *Lespagnandelle*
42. Callipygean Venus, by *Clérion*
43. Silenus with the child Bacchus, by *Mazière*
44. Antinous Belvedere, by *Le Gros*
45. Farnese Mercury, by *Mélo*
46. Urania, by *Carlier* or *Granier*
47. Apollo Belvedere, by *Mazeline*

NORTH SLOPE
48. Melancholy, by *La Perdrix*
49. Antinous Belvedere, by *Lacroix*
50. Barbarian Prisoner, by *André*
51. Faun playing a Flute, by *Hurtrelle*
52. Medici Bacchus, by *Granier*
53. Faustina, by *Regnaudin*
54. Commodus as Hercules, by N. *Coustou*
55. Urania, by *Frémery*
56. Ganymede, by *Laviron*
    Statues 39, 40 and 48 were part of the Great Commission of 1674

List of the Sculptures

PARTERRE OF LATONA

STAIRCASE

57. The central avenue of the Water Parterre ends at this staircase.

Flanking the top of the staircase
58. Sun Vase, by *Drouilly*
59. Sun Vase, by *Du Goulon*

Above the Fountain of Latona,
4 marble vases by *Grimaud*
60. 61. Vases bordered in ivy and oak leaf motifs
62. 63. Covered vases decorated with vines and masks of satyrs

FOUNTAIN OF LATONA

The pool is oval in shape. A pyramid-like structure rises out of the centre. It consists of four circular tiers, each covered in coloured marble. The sculptures are by the *Marsy* brothers. On the water surrounding the base are lead turtles and lizards. On the first level: partly-transformed peasants and frogs. On the second and third levels: frogs. On the top level we see Latona imploring Jupiter, with her two children, Apollo and Diana. This marble group is by *Balthazar Marsy*

TERRACE

Eight marble vases
64. 66. 68. Borghese vases (Bacchanal), by *Cornu*
67. 69. 71. Medici vases (Sacrifice of Iphigenia), by *Cornu*
65. Vase depicting Mars' childhood, by *Prou*
70. Vase depicting Mars' childhood, by *Hardy*

LAWNS AND FLOWERBEDS OF LATONA

72. 73. The Lizard Fountains, by the *Marsy* brothers.
In each fountain, 2 "Lycian peasants" picking reeds illustrate this same legend of metamorphosis.

HALF-MOON OF THE PARTERRE OF LATONA

74. Dying Gladiator, by *Mosnier*
75. Circe, by *Magnier*
76. Plato, by *Rayol*
77. Mercury, by *Van Clève*
78. Pandora, by *Le Gros*
79. Achelous, by *Mazière*
80. Castor and Pollux, group, by *Coysevox*
81. Paetus and Arria, group, by *Lespingola*
82. Laocoon and his sons, group, by *Tubi*
83. Papyrius and his mother, group, by *Carlier* and *Mosnier*
84. Hercules, by *Le Comte*
85. Bacchante, by *Dedieu*
86. Faun, by *Houzeau*
87. Diogenes, by *Lespagnandelle*
88. Ceres, by *Poulletier* after *Girardon*
89. Nymph with a shell, after *Coysevox*

SOUTH QUINCUNX

The majority of the terms in the Quincunxes were carved for Vaux-le-Vicomte from models by *Poussin*.

90. Morpheus
91. Flora
92. Hercules
93. Pomona
94. Reaper
95. Bacchante or Maenad
96. Vertumnus
97. Minerva

NORTH QUINCUNX

98. Flora
99. Pan
100. Liberality
101. Faun
102. Ceres
103. Bacchus
104. Abundance
105. Winter

GREEN CARPET

NORTH AVENUE
106. Geometric vase, once adorned with fleurs-de-lis in a diamond pattern, by *Herpin*
107. Cunning, by *Le Comte*, after a drawing by *Mignard*
108. Juno, classical statue discovered at Smyrna and restored by *Mazière*
109. Vase decorated with flowering cornucopia, by *Barrois*
110. Vase with wide fluting, adorned with Apollonian flowers, by *Drouilly*
111. Hercules and Telephus, by *Jouvenet*
112. Medici Venus, by *Frémery*
113. Sunflower vase, by *Legeret* or *Slodtz*
114. Fluted vase with acanthus leaves, by *Arcis*
115. Cyparissus and his deer, by *Flamen*
116. Artemisia, by *Lefèvre* and *Desjardins*
117. Vase with oak and laurel branches, once adorned with the King's monogram, by *Hardy*

List of the Sculptures

GREEN CARPET

SOUTH AVENUE
118. Geometric vase,
 once adorned with fleurs-de-lis
 in the diamond pattern, by *Poulletier*
119. Fidelity, by *Lefèvre*,
 after a drawing by *Mignard*
120. Venus rising from the sea,
 also known as the "Richelieu Venus",
 by *Le Gros*
121. Vase decorated with flowering cornucopia,
 by *Rayol*
122. Vase with wide fluting adorned with
 Apollonian flowers, by *Mélo*
123. Faun with kid, by *Flamen*
124. Dido, by *Poulletier*
125. Sunflower vase, by *Legeret*
 or *Slodtz*
126. Vase with fluting and acanthus leaves,
 by *Joly*
127. Amazon, by *Buirette*
128. Achilles at Scyros, by *Vigier*
129. Vase with oak and laurel branches,
 once adorned with the King's monogram,
 by *Hardy*

FOUNTAIN OF APOLLO

Immense quadrilobate pool.
In the centre, once-gilded lead group:
Apollo riding his chariot,
by *Jean-Baptiste Tubi*.
Facing the rising sun, the chariot, pulled by four spirited horses, emerges from the water. It is surrounded by four tritons and four dolphins.

HALF-MOON WEST
OF THE FOUNTAIN OF APOLLO

ON THE SOUTH
130. Bacchus, classical statue restored
 by *Duseigneur* in 1853
131. Pomona, by *Le Hongre*
132. Bacchus, by *Raon*
133. Spring, by *Arcis*
 and *Mazière*
134. The god Pan, by *Mazière*,
 after *Girardon*
135. Ino and Melicertes, by *Granier*,
 after *Girardon*

ON THE NORTH
136. Aristaeus and Proteus, by *Slodtz*,
 after *Girardon*
137. Syrinx, by *Mazière*
138. Jupiter, by *Clérion*
139. Juno, by *Clérion*
140. Vertumnus, by *Le Hongre*
141. Silenus holding the child Bacchus,
 classical work

APOLLO AVENUES
AT THE GRAND CANAL

SOUTH
142. Roman figure, classical statue
143. Bacchus, 18th century copy
 of a classical original
144. Farnese Hercules, classical statue
145. Woman with child, classical statue
146. Hercules, modern statue,
 by *Grégoire*, 1926
147. Juno, after a classical original

NORTH
148. Roman emperor, classical statue
149. Bacchus, modern statue
 by *Grégoire*, 1926
150. Apollo with a lyre, classical statue
151. Daylight, by *Baldi*
152. Roman figure, classical statue
153. Cleopatra, Italian School,
 end of 16th century

GRAND CANAL

Dug between 1667 and 1680. It is 200 feet wide and 5362 feet long. It has a 3290-foot arm which runs from the former Menagerie to the Grand Trianon.

GROVE OF THE DOMES

Composed of two marble balustrades. The first (circular, and adorned with weapons from various nations), encircles the second, which is hexagonal and, in turn, surrounds a pool with a marble basin in the centre.
154. Ino, by *Rayol*
155. Daybreak, by *Le Gros*
156. Acis, by *Tubi*
157. Dawn, by *Magnier*
158. Galatea, by *Tubi*
159. Amphitrite (pedestal only)
160. Arion with his lyre, by *Raon*
161. Nymph of Diana, by *Flamen*

162. Marble vase decorated with musical instruments and garlands of flowers,
 by *Robert*

FOUNTAIN OF ENCELADUS

A circular pool bordered with grass, frequently called "Enceladus." In the centre lies a Giant, half-crushed under a pile of rocks; also called "The Engulfed." Lead sculpture by *G. Marsy*.

List of the Sculptures

OBELISK

Two-level octagonal pool.
The lower edge is rounded on two sides and surrounded by a raised moat and a three-level base.
A cone-shaped jet of water rises from a clump of reeds in the centre.

163. 164. Small curved pedestals

FOUNTAIN OF FLORA

165. Fountain of Flora or Spring
In the centre of a circular pool: island of spring strewn with flowers; Flora and four cupids. Lead sculpture by *Tubi*.

STAR GROVE

Formerly the Grove of the Water Mountain.
Shaded, with radiating walks
166. 167. 168. 169. 170. Empty pedestals.
171. Bacchante, classical work

FOUNTAIN OF CERES

172. Fountain of Ceres, or Summer
In the centre of an octagonal pool: island of summer covered with harvest sheaves, Ceres and three cupids. Lead sculpture by *Regnaudin*

BATHS OF APOLLO

Located in a clearing surrounded by thickets and tall trees. Next to a small lake, a grotto is dug out of a rock. Called the Palace of Tethys, it was created in the 18th century by *Hubert Robert*.
In the center of the rock: group representing Apollo tended by the nymphs. Apollo and three nymphs by *Girardon*, and three nymphs to the rear, by *Regnaudin*.
Below, groups of Sun Horses being groomed by tritons. Rearing horse by *Marsy*, drinking horse by *Guérin*.

GREEN RING

Formerly the Water Theatre Grove
173. Dancing Faun (pedestal only)
174. Pomona
175. Ganymede
176. Ceres
177. The Island of Children Fountain. Circular pool with lead rims. In the centre six children sit on a rock, two others play in the water. Once-gilded lead sculptures by *Hardy*.
178. Health (Hygia)
179. Adrian (pedestal only)

FOUNTAIN OF NEPTUNE

180. Faustina, by *Frémery*
181. The Glory of the King, by *Domenico Guidi*
182. Berenice, by *Lespingola*
183. Sea dragon ridden by a cupid, by *Bouchardon*
184. Proteus leaning on a sea-unicorn, by *Bouchardon*
185. Neptune and Amphitrite, by *Lambert-Sigisbert Adam*
186. Oceanus riding on sea animals, by *Jean-Baptiste Lemoine*
187. Sea dragon ridden by a cupid, by *Bouchardon*
Twenty-two lead vases decorated with aquatic figures adorn the coping of the channel. They border the retaining wall, decorated with lead masks and shells, on the south side.

DRAGON FOUNTAIN

Large circular pool. A clawed dragon with bat-like wings is surrounded by four fleeing mythical fish. Four children riding on swans attack the monster with their bows. Lead sculptures by the *Marsy* brothers, redone by *Tony Noël* (1889)

WATER AVENUE

In a small circular basin, bronze children in groups of three hold aloft a pink marble bowl.
188. Three little girls, by *Buirette*
189. Three little boys, by *Buirette*
190. Three children playing with fish, by *Mazeline*
191. Three hunters, by *Mazeline*
192. Three children playing with fish, by *Mazeline*
193. Three hunters, by *Mazeline*
194. Three little boys, by *Buirette*
195. Three little girls, by *Buirette*
196. Three terms, by *Lerambert*
197. Three satyrs, by *Le Gros*
198. Three child musicians, by *Lerambert*
199. Boys and girl dancing, by *Lerambert*
200. Cupids and little girl, by *Le Hongre*
201. Three dancers, by *Le Gros*
202. Three tritons, by *Le Gros*

BATHING NYMPHS

203. Square pool, decorated on three sides with bas-reliefs in lead by *Le Hongre, Le Gros* and *Girardon*. The famous "Diana's Bathing Nymphs" by *Girardon* is on the northern wall.

List of the Sculptures

GROVE OF THE TRIUMPHAL ARCH

Situated east of the Water Avenue, this grove takes its name from "an arch in gilded ironwork," no longer in existence. A part of the group "France in Triumph" remains. Captives in lead by *Tubi* and *Coysevox*.

GROVE OF THE THREE FOUNTAINS

The slope west of the Water Avenue was the setting for a series of fountains and pools, no longer in existence.

PYRAMID

204. Circular pool with marble rim. In the centre, four superimposed lead bowls.
Bowl 1 held by 4 large tritons
Bowl 2 held by young tritons
Bowl 3 held by dolphins
Bowl 4 held by crayfish
Lead vase at the top.
Designed by *Le Brun*
Pyramid carved by *Girardon*

NORTH PARTERRE

WEST AVENUE
205. Europe, by *Mazeline*
206. Africa, by *Cornu*
207. Night, by *Raon*
208. Earth, by *Massou*
209. The Pastoral Poem, by *Granier*

CROSSROADS OF THE PHILOSOPHERS
210. Ulysses, by *Magnier*
211. Isocrates, by *Granier*
212. Theophrastus, by *Hurtrelle*
213. Lysias, by *Dedieu*
214. Apollonius, by *Mélo*

NORTH AVENUE
215. Autumn, by *Regnaudin*
216. America, by *Guérin*
217. Summer, by *Hutinot*
218. Winter, by *Girardon*
219. Choler, by *Houzeau*
220. Blood, by *Jouvenet*
221. The Satirical Poem, by *Buyster*
222. Asia, by *Roger*
223. Phlegm, by *Lespagnandelle*
224. The Epic Poem, by *Drouilly*

LOWER PARTERRE
225. Two marble vases decorated with children playing

226. 227. CROWN FOUNTAINS
In each circular pool two mermaids and two tritons swim around a laurel wreath. Lead sculptures by *Tubi* and *Le Hongre*.
228. Marble vase with grape motif, by *Cornu*
229. Two marble vases encircled with oak branches, by *Bertin*
230. Marble vase with grape motif, by *Cornu*

RECTILINEAR COPING
Overhanging the wall bordering the South Parterre
A. B. Twelve bronze vases after *Ballin*. Six models are arranged symmetrically. Heads of fauns, cupids, snarling wolves, mermaids, country and sea gods form the handles.
231. Two identical vases in Egyptian marble, by *Rousseau* and *Mazière*

MAIN STAIRCASE
Flanked by two bronze statues
232. The Knife-Grinder (L'Arrotino), by *Foggini*
233. Kneeling Venus, by *Coysevox*
234. Two similar bronze vases adorned with sun faces and encircled with classical silhouettes in medallions, by *Michel Anguier*
235. Marble vase bordered with vine branches, with rams' head handles, by *Hurtrelle*

SOUTH PARTERRE

Flower beds laid out symmetrically on either side of a central avenue surround plain circular pools.
236. Ariadne sleeping or Cleopatra, by *Van Clève*
C. Nine bronze vases cast by *Calla*
237. 238. Marble vases with dolphins forming the handles
239. 240. Marble vases, by *Tubi* and *Hulot*
D. Six bronze vases cast by *Duval*
241. 242. Cupids carried by sphinxes, in bronze and marble, by *Lerambert* and *Sarrazin*
E. Six vases in bronze cast by *Duval*
243. 244. Marble vases, with fauns' heads forming the handles, by *Bertin*
F. Nine vases in bronze cast by *Calla*
245. Marble vase, Sacrifice to Bacchus, by *Bertin*
246. Marble vase, Roman funeral, by *Bertin*
C.D.E.F. These bronze vases with young satyrs, cupids, dragons and mermaids forming the handles, are after models by *Claude Ballin*, a famous goldsmith during the reign of Louis XIV. Vases in the A and B series are also after *Ballin*.

List of the Sculptures

ORANGERY

247. 248. Marble vases with a Dionysian theme

THE HUNDRED STEPS

249. Aurora and Cephalus, by *Le Gros*
250. Vertumnus and Pomona, by *Le Gros*
251. Zephyr and Flora, by *Le Comte*
252. Venus and Adonis, by *Le Comte*

The Orangery Parterre surrounds a plain circular pool.

QUEEN'S GROVE

This replaced the Labyrinth Grove "which was decorated with fountains containing coloured lead animals illustrating Aesop's fables."

253. Fighting Gladiator, in bronze, after a classical original in the Louvre (Borghese Collection)
254. Bust of a Bacchant
255. Bust of a young girl
256. Bust of a young man
257. Bust of a Roman woman
258. Medici Venus in bronze
259. Minerva in polychrome marble

ROCKWORK GROVE

Also called the Ballroom. A central platform was once covered with marble for dancing. The spectators stood on steps near the entrances, facing rockwork bowl tiers decorated with shells.
Above, vases in gilded lead by *Le Hongre* and *Le Comte*.
Gilded lead candlestands with musical motifs stand on marble pedestals between the lower tiers. The candlestands are by *Massou, Jouvenet, Le Gros* and *Mazeline*.

260. Marsyas and Olympus, after a classical original.

FOUNTAIN OF BACCHUS

261. Fountain of Bacchus or Autumn
In the centre of an octagonal pool: island of autumn covered with grapes. Bacchus and four little satyrs, lead sculpture, by *B.* and *G. Marsy*.

WATER MIRROR

Unadorned pool bordered with grass, it was the "upper pool, in a farthingale shape in the Grove of the Royal Island."

262. Marble vase bordered with ivy, by *Lefèvre*
263. Woman in drapery, classical original
264. Apollo-Pothos, classical original
265. Half-dressed Venus, classical original
266. Woman in draped garment, classical original
267. Marble vase bordered with ivy, by *Legeret*

KING'S GARDEN

An English garden which replaced the large pool of the Royal Island in the 19th century.

268. Marble vase in honour of Bacchus
269. Marble vase with funeral motif
270. Farnese Flora, by *Raon*
271. Farnese Hercules, by *Cornu*

FOUNTAIN OF SATURN

272. Fountain of Saturn, or Winter
In the centre of a circular pool: island of winter, border edged with icicles and covered with shells.
An aging, winged Saturn and four cupids, lead sculpture by *Girardon*

COLONNADE

Built by *Mansart* and *Le Nôtre*.
Grove with marble colonnade.
Thirty-two columns support a circular cornice resting on small flying buttresses, in turn resting on thirty-two square pilasters. Twenty-eight marble basins are set between the columns.
The spandrels are adorned with bas-reliefs representing childhood.

273. Site of the famous group by *Girardon*, the Rape of Persephone by Pluto
274. Marble vase adorned with garlands of flowers and musical instruments, by *Robert*

HALL OF CHESTNUT TREES

Formerly the Hall of Classical Statues

275. Round pool with white marble bowl
276. Marcus Aurelius (bust)
277. Otho (bust)
278. Antinous (removed)
279. Alexander (bust)
280. Apollo (bust)
281. Round pool with white marble bowl
282. Antoninus (bust)
283. Septimius Severus (bust)
284. Meleager (after the classical work in the Vatican)
285. Octavian (bust)
286. Hannibal (bust)

COMMENTARY ON THE PLATES

*Each description includes, on the left,
a number corresponding to the illustrated page;
on the right, a number corresponding to the list and map.*

♦ *Cross-reference to numbers in left-hand column.*

| Page references | Map references | Page references | Map references |

Versailles and the French Garden

17 NYMPH WITH PEARLS — 11
This beautiful face belongs to a nymph reclining on the rim of the South Pool. She has taken a tiara and a pearl necklace from a shell held out to her by a cupid. This work is an elegant masterpiece in the tradition of "Diana the Huntress" at Anet. Etienne Le Hongre was paid for the clay model between 1684 and 1688.
♦ 230-239

18 ARIADNE SLEEPING, OR CLEOPATRA — 236
Acquired by Pope Julius II, this classical work was admired by artists and extolled by poets in the 16th and 17th centuries. It was first known as "Cleopatra," but at the end of the 18th century it became "The Abandoned Ariadne Sleeping." It is a shame we do not know the original sculptor of this graceful work, dating from the 3rd century B.C.
François I had a cast of this statue made by Primaticcio for the Château of Fontainebleau, where it stood near Laocöon and the Belvedere Apollo. Between 1684 and 1685 Corneille Van Clève used this cast to carve the marble Ariadne for Versailles. At the same time, the King had a copy of the original made in Rome by Jean-Baptiste Goy. It was created for the Meudon Gardens but is no longer in existence.

19 BACCHUS — 149
A modern copy (1926) by René Grégoire of the classical work originally placed in this spot and accidentally broken in 1863.

20 CASTOR AND POLLUX — 80
21
The original classical work from the Ludovisi Collection was sold in 1678 to Queen Christina of Sweden, then living in Rome. After belonging to various collectors, it was acquired by Philip V of Spain (grandson of Louis XIV) in 1724 for the San Ildefonso Palace, and from there it was moved to the Prado Museum in 1839.
The copy for Versailles by Antoine Coysevox (1640-1720) was made between 1685 and 1712. It was first placed in the Hall of Classical Statues, and, in 1712, at the entrance to the Green Carpet.
This statue is signed "A. COYZEVOX 1712". In the 17th century, the group was identified as Castor and Pollux. Since then, however, authors like Pierre de Nolhac have noticed that the symbolic elements have been restored arbitrarily, putting the identity of the figures in question.
Height: 7'7".

22 BRONZE VASES — Map
23 IN THE SOUTH PARTERRE
Claude Ballin (1615-1678), Louis XIV's famous goldsmith, furnished the models for these vases as well as for the 12 bronze vases on the copings overhanging the south side of the North Parterre. The South Parterre is surrounded by thirty bronze vases. Twelve of them are arranged in sets of six on the north side. They are separated by the main staircase leading to the parterre. Though a detailed description of each vase will not be given, we can mention the six key motifs which differentiate them:
—Dragons and scenes from the Apollo legend
—Janus' Heads
—Lion's heads
—Sphinxes
—Satyrs
—Signs of the zodiac.
These motifs are repeated symmetrically.
The twelve vases were cast between 1765 and 1769 by Duval.
Eighteen vases are arranged more or less symmetrically in sets of nine on two copings along the east and west edges of the parterre. The following motifs can be distinguished:
—Mermaids and Bacchus' retinue
—Fauns with long horns
—Cupids
—Masks and fluting
—Sphinxes
—Satyrs
—Janus
—Lion's heads
—Signs of the Zodiac.
All eighteen vases were cast in 1852 by Calla.

24 VIEW OF THE CHATEAU — Map
25 FROM THE WATER PARTERRE
The projecting main building is referred to as "the central section." It is part of the "envelope" built by Louis Le Vau around Louis XIII's brick and stone hunting lodge and was constructed between 1668 and 1671.
Originally, the west façade of the "envelope" had a terrace separating the King's Apartment on the left, to the north, from the Queen's Apartment on the right, to the south. It was an Italian-style palace, entirely in stone, with the three orders (Ionic, Doric and Corinthian) superimposed. Le Vau designed the roof with a false terrace surrounded by a balustrade, richly decorated with sculpted trophies and vases.
In 1678, the King accepted Jules Hardouin-Mansart's project to link the sections, by removing the terrace and creating space for the Hall of Mirrors and the War and Peace Drawing Rooms. The Dauphin's apartment was placed in the old section, on the south side of the ground floor. Louis XIV's sumptuous Bathing Apartment was located at the opposite end. The Lower Gallery, situated between the two, led directly to the gardens from the Marble Courtyard.
Since Louis XV had many children, the Bathing Apartment had to be redecorated and gradually took over the Lower Gallery; it was converted into apartments for his daughters. Marie-Antoinette obtained the apartment in the centre belonging to Madame Sophie de France after her aunt's death, and had it made into a private apartment for herself and her children. Little of it remains, as it was destroyed by Louis-Philippe.
To the right of the central section is the South Wing, reserved for princes of the blood. Mansart began construction here in 1678.
The North Wing, begun in 1685, lies on the other side. The garden side was reserved for important courtiers. The roof of the chapel by Mansart and Robert de Cotte (1699-1710) tops this wing.
Two large expanses of water, referred to as the "Water Parterre," lie in front of the central section. A number of bronze groups were placed there in 1690. They represent the rivers of France, and alternate with groups of nymphs and groups of children at the corners.

TETRALOGIES

26   ASIA   222
Carved by Léonard Roger after drawings by Charles Le Brun. Le Brun himself was inspired by Ripa's "Iconologia."
The young woman personifying Asia holds a perfume-brazier with a jewelled turban at her feet.
The statue was part of the "Great Commission of 1674" and was executed between 1675 and 1680. White marble. Height: over 6'.
♦ 27

27   THE GREAT COMMISSION OF 1674
A series of twenty-four statues grouped in this book under the theme "Tetralogies."
The year 1674 marked the completion of both the stone "envelope" built by Louis Le Vau around Louis XIII's hunting lodge and the Fountains of the Seasons. The new double perspective of the gardens called for sculpted decoration. Thus, the Water Parterre, with its arabesque decor, was laid out in front of the central section, beneath the terrace Mansart later enclosed to build the Hall of Mirrors. In 1674, the idea came about to decorate Le Nôtre's curved pool with a set of twenty-four white marble statues. This was the famous "Great Commission of 1674," suggested to Louis XIV by Colbert and carried out under the close supervision of Charles Le Brun over the next ten years. In addition to these twenty-four statues (the Continents, the Seasons, the Humours, the Four Types of Poetry, the Four Parts of the Day and the Elements) four colossal groups known as the "Rapes" were planned. (Only "The Rape of Persephone," carved by Girardon, remains in the Versailles collection.)
It seems that these white statues, measuring over six feet in height (not including the pedestals), interfered with the view of the Green Carpet and the Grand Canal, from the Water Parterre. It was then that the Water Parterre was modified to its present-day format. In addition to this, as we know, Colbert's influence with the King diminished from 1671 (and consequently Le Brun's as well), as Louvois, Mignard's benefactor, stepped in. For these political but above all aesthetic reasons, the twenty-four statues were finally placed near the château, mainly in the hedge niches surrounding the North Parterre, after 1683, the year of Colbert's death and the destruction of the original Water Parterre.
Three of the four "Rapes" originally intended for the four corners of the Water Parterre were completed and set in place. "The Rape of Oreithyia" (begun by Marsy and completed by Flamen) and the "Rape of Cybele by Saturn" by Regnaudin went to the Orangery Parterre in 1687. "The Rape of Persephone by Pluto," Girardon's masterpiece, was placed in the centre of the Colonnade Grove upon its completion in 1699. Only "The Rape of Coronis by Neptune" never saw the light of day.

27   AMERICA   216
This work by Gilles Guérin (1609-1678) was carved between 1675 and 1678, after a drawing by Charles Le Brun, as part of the "Great Commission."
She is quaintly attired in a skirt and wears a feather headdress. The bow and arrow she carries tells us that men and women alike fought in that country. A severed head lies at her feet, "to show how this inhuman people feeds on human flesh." There is also a crocodile "so ferocious in that country that it devours other animals and even men."
White marble. Height: 6'10".
♦ 49

28   AIR   31
Executed by Étienne Le Hongre (1628-1690), after a drawing by Charles Le Brun, between 1680 and 1684.
This is undoubtedly one of the masterpieces of the "Great Commission". The sculptor had mastered the art of classical statuary and Bernini's baroque technique which he had studied while in Rome from 1653 to 1659.
Air is represented by a beautiful woman with bare breast. An eagle with spread wings sits next to her. The billowing fabric over her head suggests the flow of air. The wind flattens it against her legs, making it billow out behind. Movement is suggested harmoniously without the exaggeration so typical of Berninesque baroque.
White marble. Height: 6'10".
♦ 27

29   FIRE   40
This element is part of the "Great Commission," and was done between 1675 and 1684 by Nicolas Dossier, after a drawing by Charles Le Brun.
A woman holding a brazier in her left hand embodies Fire. At her feet is a salamander.
White marble. Height: 7'2".
♦ 27

30   WATER   37
32
This statue was carved by Pierre Legros (1629-1714) between 1675 and 1681. He faithfully followed Le Brun's drawing.
This woman radiates health and spirit, and the work is both original and modern in feeling. We are almost certain that the face is that of the artist's wife, Jeanne Marsy, sister of the famous sculptors.
White marble. Height: 6'6".
♦ 27

31   EARTH   208
33
Sculpted in 1681 by Benoît Massou (1627-1684), after a drawing by Le Brun, this work was part of the "Great Commission."
Massou reduced the number of symbols recommended by Ripa to a minimum.
Earth is represented as a beautiful woman with flowers in her hair. A loosely-draped robe gives her a majestic air. She is holding a horn of plenty in her left hand while the lion at her feet looks up at her. According to Ripa, she is the mother of all animals.
White marble. Height: 7'2".
♦ 27

Tetralogies

34 / 35 — NIGHT — 207
Carved by Jean Raon (1630-1707) in 1680, after a drawing by Le Brun, as part of the "Great Commission."
Although a relatively easy subject to treat on canvas, night can be extremely difficult to render in stone. Raon did not achieve the miraculous. Seeking to portray "night at the moment she retires" (Ripa), he attempted to infuse movement into the marble. The pose, however, is rather static.
White marble. Height: 6'6".
♦ 27

36 — DAYBREAK — 35
Daybreak (or Dawn) was carved by Gaspard Marsy (1629-1681) at the same time as "Venus" or "Noon," after a drawing by Le Brun, between 1676 and 1680. The figure is a young woman who appears to be moving forward wearing a star on her head, "indicating the light that Dawn brings us" (Ripa). It is one of the Four Parts of Day from the "Great Commission."
Height: 7'2".
♦ 27

37 — VENUS, OR NOON — 33
A model of grace and elegance created by Gaspard Marsy between 1676 and 1680 after a drawing by Le Brun. Part of the "Great Commission."
The sculptor remained faithful to Ripa: "Venus depicted here with her son, Cupid, burns and wounds those she touches with her flames and arrows... Even the blazing sun does not burn with such ardour".
Height: 6'6'.
♦ 27

38 / 39 — DIANA, OR EVENING — 32
Carved in white marble by Martin Desjardins (1637-1694), between 1675 and 1684, after a drawing by Le Brun. Part of the "Great Commission."
The famous "Diana and her Doe" or "Versailles Diana" from the royal collections inspired this work. Louis XIV had it placed in a niche in the Hall of Mirrors, and since the Revolution it has been in the Louvre. (Attributed to Leochares, a contemporary of Lysippus, 4th century B.C.)
The Diana by Desjardins seems less resolute in spirit that her classical model. The sculptor gave her a finer silhouette and a softer pose.
Height: approximately 6'6".
♦ 27

40 / 41 — SUMMER — 217
Begun by Pierre Hutinot (1616-1679) and completed by his son between 1675 and 1679, after a drawing by Charles Le Brun. Part of the "Great Commission."
The goddess Ceres represents summer. Her right hand holds a sickle and her left rests on a sheaf of wheat. Hutinot followed Le Brun's drawing faithfully, and it shows up in this rather heavy sculpture.
White marble. Height: 7'6".
♦ 27-57-70-74-79-255

42 — AUTUMN — 215
Carved by Thomas Regnaudin (1622-1706) between 1680 and 1694. The sculptor chose to represent this season as the harvest god, Bacchus, and not Vulcan, as Ripa would have recommended. Crowned with vine leaves, the god raises a cup in his left hand. A basket of grapes rests at his feet. One of the Seasons from the "Great Commission."
White marble. Height: approximately 6'10".
♦ 27-95-173-184-240

42 / 43 — WINTER — 218
A masterpiece of 17th century art by François Girardon (1628-1715), after a drawing by Charles Le Brun, executed between 1675 and 1686.
Girardon chose not to follow Ripa's instructions and used the old French allegories for the months. We find such allegories in cathedral decor, and, as Francastel has observed, in the work of Jean Goujon at the former Hôtel de Ligneris.
In the French tradition, this bearded old man, warming himself over a brazier, was used to illustrate February and March. The contours of his body are as magnificent as his facial expression: that of an old man, a pauper, frozen to the bone.
White marble. Height: approximately 7'6".
♦ 27-110-131

44 / 45 — SPRING — 36
By Philippe Magnier (1647-1715), who, under Le Brun's instructions, portrayed this season as a beautiful, gracious young woman holding a basket of flowers. Carved between 1675 and 1681, this statue from the "Great Commission" is the goddess Flora.
Height: approximately 6'6".
♦ 27-57-62-135

46 — EUROPE — 205
Executed as part of the "Great Commission" by Pierre Mazeline (1632-1708) from 1675 to 1680, after a drawing by Charles Le Brun. Europe is portrayed as a helmeted woman leaning on a shield with a rearing horse motif.
White marble. Height: 7'6".
♦ 27

47 — AFRICA — 206
Begun by Georges Sibrayque (?-1694) and finished by Jean Cornu (1650-1710) after the former's death. Carved as part of the "Great Commission," it is an original and modern work slightly deviating from the classical statuary tradition. Her headdress, made from an elephant head, may have been inspired by a medallion of the Emperor Hadrian (76-138). The "Comptes des Bâtiments du Roi" mention that the work was begun in 1682 by Sibrayque and that the last payments received by Cornu were dated 1694.
White marble. Height: 6'10".
♦ 27

48 — ASIA — 222
♦ 27

49 — AMERICA — 216
♦ 27

The Seasons

50 MELANCHOLY — **48**
One of man's four Humours, carved by Michel de La Perdrix (circa 1641-1681) after a drawing by Le Brun, for the "Great Commission," between 1675 and 1680.
La Perdrix faithfully followed the drawing by Le Brun, who himself had consulted ripa. This Humour is a man, whose mouth is covered with a strip of cloth, showing his preference for "solitude and silence." The closed pouch in his right hand symbolizes avarice, and the book, his love of study.
White marble. Height: 7'6".
♦ 27

50 PHLEGM — **223**
From the Humours series.
Carved in 1675 by Mathieu Lespagnandelle (1616-1689) after a drawing by Charles Le Brun. Both the badger fur the man is wearing and the turtle at his feet symbolize laziness. The crossed arms suggest a man who has no desire to do anything.
White marble. Height: 7'6".
♦ 27

51 CHOLER — **219**
Executed between 1675 and 1680 by Jacques Houzeau (1624-1691) after a drawing by Le Brun. This Humour is illustrated by a furious man, his arm upraised, accompanied by a roaring lion. The iconography here is in perfect keeping with Le Brun's ideas about the parallel between the expressions of man and of animals.
White marble. Height: 7'6".
♦ 27

51 BLOOD — **220**
This work was executed between 1675 and 1680 by Noël Jouvenet (1644-1717), and was part of the "Great Commission." It faithfully follows Ripa's principles of "Iconology," as do the other "Humours of Man." It is a man playing a flute (an homage to Venus and Bacchus), accompanied by a billy goat "nibbling on a bunch of grapes," a symbol of luxury. It is pendant to Choler.
White marble. Height: 7'4".
♦ 27

52 THE EPIC POEM — **224**
Sculpted between 1675 and 1679 by Jean Drouilly (?-1698), after a drawing by Le Brun, according to Ripa's manual.
This type of poetry is represented by a man standing dressed in a short tunic and a cloak draped over his shoulders. He is wearing a laurel wreath (a symbol of victory) and holds the trumpet of fame in his left hand. It has been said that his face is that of Louis XIV when young.
White marble. Height: 7'4".
♦ 27

52 THE PASTORAL POEM — **209**
This work, begun by Gérard-Léonard Hérard (rough-hewn from a marble block), was carved by Pierre Granier (1635-1715) between 1675 and 1680 as part of the "Great Commission." A shepherdess crowned with wildflowers was chosen to represent this poem. A scrip, used by shepherds to carry bread, is attached to her waist. She holds Pan's flute in her left hand and leans on a walking-stick with her right.
White marble. Height: 7'6".
♦ 27

53 THE SATIRICAL POEM — **221**
Philippe Buyster (1595-1688) executed this work after a drawing by Charles Le Brun. The statue was set in place in 1681 and was part of the "Great Commission." It portrays a man leaning on a stick covered with ivy. We can read cunning and mockery into his sarcastic smile.
White marble. Height: about 6'10".
♦ 27

53 THE LYRIC POEM — **39**
Carved by Jean-Baptiste Tubi (1635-1700) in 1682, after a drawing by Charles Le Brun; it was part of the "Great Commission."
A beautiful woman crowned with laurel plucks the strings of a lyre, the favourite instrument of Apollo. According to Greek legend, he was the god of music and poetry.
White marble. Height: 6'10".
♦ 27

SPRING

54 THE ANTINOUS BELVEDERE — **44**
Carved by Pierre Legros (1629-1714) in 1684 after a cast in the classical statue reserve.
Legros completed the right arm, which is missing in the original. (Classical original in the Vatican Museum, Belvedere.) Today, however, it is no longer considered as an Antinous, but as a Hermes from the Praxiteles School (4th century B.C.)
Height: 7'6".
Most of the statues adorning the two slopes forming the "horseshoe" around the Parterre of Latona were executed after classical originals. Two figures reclining at the foot of the Parterre complete the statuary on these slopes.
♦ 29-50-53-63-114-138-139-141-148-149-160-161

55 NORTH AND SOUTH QUINCUNXES — **101**
THE TERMS
On April 9, 1684, Louis XIV arranged to buy eleven white marble terms from the Comte de Vaux (son of Fouquet, his former minister who had been imprisoned for 23 years and was to die that year). These terms were much smaller than those in the Latona Half-Moon and the Fountain of Apollo, but their origin was quite impressive. Each one was purchased for 1,800 livres. The King made quite a bargain, given that the models were made by Nicolas Poussin (1594-1665), the greatest French painter of the 17th century!

The Seasons

According to letters which have been preserved, around 1655 Nicolas Fouquet asked his brother, the abbot Louis Fouquet, then living in Rome, to contact Poussin. It was then that the painter made the wax models which were subsequently carved in marble and sent to Vaux-le-Vicomte.

In his "Vita degli Artisti," Bellori wrote concerning Poussin that in these terms *"Rappresento li varij Geniy de' fiori, e de' frutti dalla terra in figure di huomini, e di donne con tutto il petto humano sopra Termini, evero herme... Evvi il Dio Pane con la sampogna pastorale, coronato di pino con un ramo in mano, il Dio Fauno ridente inghirlandato d'ellera il petto, Pallade cinto l'elmo d'ulivo, con ramo nella destra, e'l serpente : Cerere, Baccho con le spiche, e l'uve, et altre ninfe, e numi con seni di fuori e di frutti, e corna d'abbondanza in contrasegno della fertile, e delitiosa villa."* *

All of the terms were carved by Théodon except for three by Domenico Guidi: Pan, Pallas and a faun. Five other terms, probably the work of Théodon, were added to the series.

Eight terms were placed in the South Quincunxes, at the site of the former Girandole Grove: Morpheus, a Reaper, Flora, a Bacchante, Pomona, Minerva, Hercules and Vertumnus. Flora, Summer, Pan, Bacchus, Abundance, Liberality, Winter and a Faun were placed in the North Quincunxes (formerly the Grove of the Dauphin). The faun on page 55 was carved by Domenico Guidi.

♦ 59-74-96-97-98-131-174-175
  176-177-182-183-185

* (In these terms Poussin) *"represents the different spirits of the flowers and fruits of the earth in the shape of men and women standing as herms, on pedestals. There is the God Pan with his pastoral musette, crowned with pine branches and a branch in his hand, the Faun God, laughing with his chest covered in ivy; Pallas, her helmet covered with olive branches, a branch in her right hand, and the serpent. Ceres holding stalks of wheat and Bacchus with grapes, other nymphs and gods carrying flowers and fruits, and the horn of plenty, a symbol of the great fertility and delight to be found at this villa."* (The Artists' Life, by Bellori.)

56 THE KING'S GARDEN → Map
This garden was created by Louis XVIII. It was known to Versailles residents and plant lovers for its calm and its flowers and trees of various, and often rare, species. The King's Garden was designed by the architect Dufour around 1817 and now occupies the site of Louis XIV's Royal Island, a large pool which gradually filled with mud due to insufficient upkeep.
♦ 60-62-75

57 THE FOUNTAIN OF FLORA 165
On May 4, 1672, Louis XIV received a letter from Colbert informing him that "models are being made for four new fountains." They were the Fountains of the Seasons, both round and octagonal in shape, with marble rims. They were situated at the intersections of the main lateral avenues of the park. The lead groups destined to adorn them had to be rather low so as not to obstruct the view. They were placed in the centre of each pool, accompanied by smaller, secondary, carved groups which quickly disappeared; others went to the Trianon. Charles Le Brun furnished the drawings for Ceres (by Regnaudin), Flora (by Tubi), Bacchus (by Marsy), and Saturn (by Girardon).

The figures were entirely gilded and the accessories were painted in natural colours. They were repainted in the same way several years ago. The Fountain of Flora (or Spring) was entrusted to Jean-Baptiste Tubi, who executed the main composition placed in the centre of a circular pool, between 1672 and 1675. The goddess leans on a basket of freshly-cut "cornflowers and anemones." Four cupids surrounding her play with a garland of flowers.
♦ 44-62-135

58 "THE QUEEN OF SWEDEN'S FAUN" 51
This statue of a faun playing the flute is a copy by Simon Hurtrelle (1648-1724) of a classical work which once belonged to Queen Christina. It first went to the Borghese Collection and was then bought by Napoleon and placed in the Louvre. It is attributed to the Praxiteles School. Another classical replica is found in the Capitoline Museum in Rome.
Hurtrelle executed his copy in 1685.
Height: 7'6".
♦ 149

58 GALATEA 158
59 Galatea is a beautiful nereid with milk-white skin. She seems to emerge from the waters to join her beloved Acis, carried by two dolphins. The sculpture by Jean-Baptiste Tubi had been carved in 1667 for the famous Grotto of Tethys, also destined to accommodate the nymphs by Girardon and Regnaudin and the Sun Horses by Marsy and Guérin. Naturally, Galatea's companion was the handsome Acis by Tubi.
Like all the statues from the Grotto of Tethys, destroyed in 1685, Galatea was often moved from place to place. In 1686, all the statues were taken to the Grove of the Domes. Acis and Galatea remained there until 1844, at which time Louis-Philippe had them sent to the park of Saint-Cloud. In 1871, the two statues returned to Versailles and were placed in the storeroom. In 1897, they were once again placed in the Grove of the Domes, on their original pedestals sculpted by Philippe Caffiéri.
Height: 5'6".
♦ 198

59 YOUNG FAUN 101
One of the terms in the North Quincunx, by Domenico Guidi, here under the shade of the blossoming chestnut trees.
♦ 55-183

60 THE KING'S GARDEN 268
The lower section of what was once the grove of 269
the Royal Island became an "English garden", with little sculpted decoration.
♦ 56-62-75

61 SILENUS AND BACCHUS 141
This group most probably came from the Marly Gardens (the Grove of Agripinna), stripped of their sculptures during the Revolution. It was then placed in the walk north of the Fountain of Apollo in 1795, replacing the statue of a senator.

The Seasons

It was made from fragments of the Greek original: Silenus' torso, as well as the body and the head of the child. This is also the case with several statues situated on the avenues of the Fountain of Apollo.
Two classical groups treating the same subject exist. One is in the Louvre (formerly in the Borghese Collection). The other, discovered in the home of Livia, wife of Augustus, on the Capitoline, is now in the Vatican Museum.
Several scholars agree that the original model was probably the work of Lysippus (latter part of the 4th century B.C.).
Height: 6'2".
♦ 144

62 THE KING'S GARDEN
Spring colours in the King's Garden.
♦ 56-60-75

→ Map

62 FLORA OR SPRING
This white marble term was begun in 1688 by Marc Arcis (1655-1739) based on a model by Girardon. It was completed by Simon Mazière and bears the inscription, "S. Mazières 1699." In 1702, it was placed in the Half-Moon of the Fountain of Apollo. Flora is crowned with flowers and holds a long garland entwined around her left arm. Remember that it was she who gave Juno a flower which could make her conceive without Jupiter's help. The god Mars was born and the Romans gave the first month of spring his name in memory of this.
Height: 6'6".
♦ 44-57-135

133

63 GANYMEDE
This group was copied in marble by Pierre Laviron (1650-1685) from a plaster cast in the classical statue reserve. The cast was made from a classical original in the Uffizi Museum in Florence. This marble piece was probably executed between 1684 and 1685.
Height: 7'6".
♦ 114-141

56

64 APRIL AT THE TRIANON
In the spring, one can see the scarlet thickets in front of the "Gardener's House" through a trellis covered in violet wisteria vines.
♦ 66-67-68-69

64 THE BELVEDERE
65
Marie-Antoinette's English-Chinese garden, designed by Hubert Robert, begins at a lake with standing water at the foot of a "mountain."
Here Richard Mique built a delightful pavilion from which the eye could take in the entire view of the new Petit Trianon gardens at a sweep. It is called the Belvedere, and was built in 1778. An octagonal pavilion with glass doors and windows, the harmony in its proportions is close to perfection. It is set on a stone platform and the steps are guarded by eight female sphinxes.
Here we see it from the "Swiss mountains," then planted with "guelder roses, paradise apples and fragrant shrubs." The Prince de Ligne, who visited this site, wrote: "I know of nothing more beautiful or more exquisitely designed than the Temple [of Love] and the Pavilion [Belvedere]. The rocks and waterfalls will soon create a breathtaking effect, for I am certain that the trees will hurry to grow and set off the pavilion, the water and the lawn."

66 THE PETIT TRIANON ORANGERY
67
In 1778-1779, Marie-Antoinette had the new Trianon Gardens enlarged. This unfortunately involved the removal of the botanical wonders of Jussieu, Linné and the Richards.
Thus, Louis XV's large botanical greenhouse was removed in 1778 and in its place Mique built the Orangery at the end of the "floral garden" facing "the Richards' House."
The Orangery which had been built in Louis XV's day was situated nearby. Marie-Antoinette used it as a theatre for festivities honouring the visit of her brother, Emperor Joseph II.
It was demolished in 1778 to make room for the rocks and the Belvedere.
♦ 64-68-69

68 THE GARDENER'S HOUSE
69
This simple and rustic building already appeared on a non-dated map during the time of Louis XV.
It was traditionally called "The Richards' House," and sometimes "The Jussieu House," after Louis XV's famous botanists, who were in charge of over four thousand plants methodically arranged according to Linné's classification.
♦ 64-66-67

SUMMER

70 THE FOUNTAIN OF CERES
On the way up the avenue to the château from the Fountain of Flora, there is an octagonal pool dedicated to Summer, or Ceres.
The central group consists of a goddess crowned with spikes of wheat, reclining on golden sheaves and surrounded by three cupids. This pool by Thomas Regnaudin, created between 1672 and 1674, after Le Brun, was the first to be completed and was finished before the Fountain of Flora.
♦ 40-57-74-79-95-110-255

172

71 SUMMER AT THE SOUTH PARTERRE
Bronze vase on the west coping of the South Parterre. The signs of the zodiac are hidden under pink geranium creepers.
♦ 22-23-76-77-79-88-89-128-129-162-248-249

→ Map

72 THE PARTERRE OF LATONA: VASES
At the foot of the parterre, on either side of the Fountain of Latona, eight large vases are placed symmetrically. These vases were carved by students at the French Academy in Rome between 1672 and 1683. They are the work of Jean Cornu, Simon Hurtrelle, Pierre Laviron and Louis Lecomte, who made six copies of the "Borghese" (Louvre) and Medici (Florence)

64
65
66
67
68
69
70
71

The Seasons

vases. The last two vases, depicting the childhood of Mars, were carved by Jacques Prou and Jean Hardy from a drawing by Mansart, between 1684 and 1688.
The "Borghese" vase acquired by Napoleon represents a bacchanal (Neo-Attic work from the first century B.C.); the "Medici" vase depicts a "sacrifice to Diana." The French sculptors took certain liberties with respect to the classical models.
Heights: from 4'10" to 6'2".
♦ 78

73 THE GRAND TRIANON
"The Marble Trianon" was built by Mansart between 1687 and 1688 after the demolition of the curious little building called the "Porcelain Trianon." It was located at the tip of the northern arm of the Grand Canal.
Although the Ionic pilasters in pink Languedoc marble were preserved, the rich sculpted decor of groups of children, vases and lead flame ornaments arranged on the balustrade of the roof were not; they were all destroyed during the Revolution.
The photograph shows the "left wing," which housed the King's second apartment from 1691 to 1703. Under Napoleon I this section was given to the Empress Marie-Louise.
During the reign of Louis XIV, the Trianon parterres and gardens were extraordinarily luxuriant. It is difficult for us to imagine them today. "We buy jars and terracotta pots... more than fourteen thousand... Then we buy shrubs, flowers, one hundred laurels, one thousand pots of white hellebores, two hundred and twenty-five jasmines, carnations, double gillyflowers, twenty thousand and fifty daffodil bulbs, one hundred and twenty-nine thousand buttercups, seven thousand eight hundred hyacinths, seventeen thousand one hundred and sixty-five tuberoses, ten thousand tulips, two thousand beautiful tulips and bulbs by the bushel, more than one hundred and sixteen..." (A. Marie).
♦ 92-93

74 CERES
Summer, personified by Ceres, is a young woman with an impish air sporting a crown of wheat. This term is probably by Théodon, after Nicolas Poussin, executed in Rome between 1679 and 1680.
♦ 40-55-70-78-182-255

75 THE KING'S GARDEN
♦ 56-60-62

76
77 BRONZE VASES
FROM THE SOUTH PARTERRE
Mermaids form the handles of the vase, while the belly is carved with scenes from the story of Bacchus.
Sphinxes crouching on lions' heads form the handles.
♦ 22-23-71-76-77-79-88-89-128-129-162-248-249

78 THE PARTERRE OF LATONA
Marble vase with bas-relief depicting the childhood of Mars, by Jacques Prou or Jean Hardy, after a drawing by Mansart.
♦ 72

79 CERES
White marble term carved by Jean Poulletier (1653-1719) between 1687 and 1688 after François Girardon.
As in the portrayals of the goddess by Regnaudin, Hutinot or Théodon, we find here the same head crowned with stalks of wheat. She holds sheaves of wheat in her left hand and a crown of wheat and cornflowers in her right.
Height: 9'1".
♦ 40-70-74

79 THE SOUTH PARTERRE
After the construction of Le Vau's "envelope" around Louis XIII's hunting lodge, the addition of the South Wing (1682) and, finally, Mansart's large Orangery (1686), the Parterre of Love looked small in comparison. Another, the same size, was built on the west and the name was changed to the "South Parterre." We have seen that the copings were adorned with bronze vases, but the four lateral staircases were decorated with marble vases carved by Bertin, Tubi and Hulot.
Though exposed to the sun, it remained an embroidered parterre with box trees and lawn for a long time, while, strangely enough, the North Parterre was already decorated with flowers. Marie Leszczynska, who could see it from her apartment windows, obtained Louis XV's permission to have it adorned with flowers as well.
♦ 22-23-76-77-84-88-89-128-129-162-248-249

80 THE NORTH PARTERRE
Around 1663 the construction of the North Parterre began under Le Nôtre's supervision. The parterres of grass bordered with shaped box trees kept their original form. Statues from the "Great Commission of 1674" were placed along the avenues in niches carved out of hedges 50 feet high. Here, as in the groves, the hedges could not withstand the harsh winters. In 1774, when Louis XVI had the gardens entirely replanted, the hedges were removed from the paths.
The photograph was taken from the north attic storey of the central section, from the apartment Madame de Pompadour used from 1745 to 1749, when she was Louis XV's mistress. In 1749 she and the King decided to become simply good friends. She then obtained the title of honorary Duchess and went to live on the ground floor of the building, keeping the same view from her windows. She died in this apartment in 1764, having remained powerful through her influence with Louis XV.
♦ 27-40-41-42-43-81-82-83-115-220-221

81 THE NORTH PARTERRE
The photograph shows the North Wing with its large slate roof covering the Opera House, at the end. The Opera was built by Gabriel for the marriage of the Dauphin and Marie-Antoinette in 1770.
♦ 27-40-80-81-82-83-115-220-221

82 VIEW OF THE NORTH PARTERRE
From the window in the North Wing, we can see the parterres in bloom and the large coping adorned with bronze vases by Ballin. Louis XIV liked to have shrubs in superimposed cone or ball shapes planted in the vases.

The Seasons

83 **NORTH PARTERRE**
This is a view of the North Wing where it meets the central section containing the royal apartments on the second floor. The Marquise-Duchesse de Pompadour spent the last twenty years of her life in the apartment on the ground floor shown here.
♦ 27-40-80-81-82-83-115-220-221

84 **VIEW OF THE SOUTH PARTERRE AND THE SOUTH AVENUE**
This view was taken from the balcony of the Queen's bedchamber. Her apartment was located on the second floor of the southern section of Le Vau's "envelope."
♦ 22-23-77-79-88-89-128-129-162

85 **THE QUEEN'S BEDCHAMBER**
Queen Maria-Theresa, the Dauphine of Bavaria, and Marie-Adelaïde, mother of Louis XV, both lived and died in this bedchamber. It was fully redecorated between 1725 and 1735 by Gabriel (father and son) for Queen Marie Leszczynska, Louis XV's wife, who lived there from 1725 until her death in 1768.
First, the fireplace was changed; then, in 1730, Le Goupil, Dugoulon, and Jacques Verberckt installed sculpted panelling next to the windows on either side of a mirror. Four years later, paintings by Natoire and de Troy were placed above the doors in homage to Queen Marie's many children: "Youth and Virtue presenting the princesses to France" and "Glory taking possession of the children of France."
Finally, in 1735, a vast project was undertaken: doors, wainscotting and mirrors were placed on the side walls, and the ceiling paintings by de Sève were removed. In their place, magnificent gold motifs were installed, and François Boucher did four monochrome paintings dedicated to the Queen's virtues: "Charity," "Abundance," "Fidelity" and "Prudence."
Upon her arrival at Versailles in 1770, Marie-Antoinette, the Dauphine, took over this apartment. The ceiling was restored and Antoine Rousseau carved the arms of France alternating with those of the House of Austria in the corners. Five years later, Marie-Antoinette was given permission to have the portraits of the parents of Queen Marie Leszczynska removed. They were replaced with tapestry portraits by Cozette of Louis XVI (between the windows), the Emperor Joseph II, Marie-Antoinette's brother (over the fireplace), and the Empress Maria-Theresa, her mother (opposite). In 1786, a Griotte marble fireplace was built there.
The fabrics (redone over the past thirty-five years in Lyons and by Paris embroiderers) are exact replicas of the silk delivered by Desfarges in 1786 "with bouquets of flowers; lilacs, roses and others with ribbons that wind round peacock feathers, creating an elegant effect." This was the "summer furnishing" that adorned the room when the Revolution reached Versailles in 1789.
Nineteen children of France were born here. Two became kings: the Duke of Anjou became Philip V of Spain in 1700 (founder of the present Spanish dynasty) and his nephew, later Louis XV, was born here in 1710.

86 **THE ORANGERY**
87 When the construction of the South Wing and the enlargement of the "embroidered" parterre were being planned, it became obvious that the little orangery built by Louis Le Vau would not be strong enough to support the weight of the new South Wing and the additional earth for the new Parterre.
It was therefore destroyed between 1684 and 1686 and Mansart built a new orangery of colossal porportions which housed a monumental gallery facing south. On each side, two immense staircases which buttress the weight of the ground and the South Wing house two lower galleries, at right angles to the first.
Le Nôtre designed the lower parterre with six curved beds. He placed it between two long arms formed by the steps, beginning at a large circular pool. In 1687 it was decided to place two of the "Rapes" from the "Great Commission" there: the "Rape of Cybele by Saturn" by Regnaudin and "The Rape of Oreithyia by Boreas" by Marsy and Flamen. They were eventually moved to the Tuileries Gardens in 1716. Both are now in the Louvre.
In 1694, bronze casts by the Kellers were apparently found there: "The Rape of Pandora by Mercury" by Jean de Boulogne, "Diana the Huntress" and "Hercules Fighting the Hydra."
Today, the classical marble original of this "Diana" is in the Louvre, but it was originally placed in the Hall of Mirrors.
The statue of Louis XIV by Desjardins, given to the King by the Maréchal de la Feuillade in 1683, was placed in a central niche inside the large gallery with its magnificent vaulted ceiling. From the top of his pedestal he could contemplate the two thousand orange trees, the one thousand oleander plants, pomegranate trees and other tropical trees placed there before the cold weather began.
Today, the only sculpted decoration in the Orangery Parterre consists of two marble vases adorned with vines and ivy, after a drawing by Mansart, executed between 1685 and 1693 by Buirette and Raon. There is, however, carved stone decoration on the pilasters along the two walks beginning at the foot of each staircase. These pilasters are topped with baskets of flowers. The walks are closed off by a grill flanked by pillars which support monumental groups: "Aurora and Cephalus" with "Vertumnus and Pomona" by Le Gros, and "Zephyr and Flora" with "Venus and Adonis" by Le Comte.
♦ 90-91

87 **STATUES ON THE ATTIC STOREY OVERLOOKING THE SOUTH PARTERRE**

88 **THE CENTRAL SECTION**
89 **SEEN FROM THE SOUTH PARTERRE**
The south façade of Le Vau's envelope, facing the South Parterre, houses the Dauphin's State Cabinet (at the corner), his library and the Dauphine's apartment.
Above, starting at the Peace Drawing Room in the corner, we can make out the windows of the Queen's apartment. During the reign of Louis XVI, the attic storey under the roof was an apartment for the Princesse de Chimay.
To the west is the façade of the Hall of Mirrors. The top storey is like a false attic; the space is

The Seasons

taken up by the hall vaulting. The rooms belonging to the Dauphin and "Mesdames de France" were on the ground floor.
♦ 22-23-71-76-77-79-84-88-89-128-129-162-248-249

90 THE ORANGERY
91 ♦ 86 → Map

92 THE PERISTYLE OF THE GRAND TRIANON
The King approved of Robert de Cotte's idea for a peristyle, much to the disapproval of Mansart, absent at the time.
Louis XIV liked the idea because it meant separating the apartments in the left and right wings, thus preventing any promiscuity. Moreover, this peristyle would allow a direct view of the garden from the parade ground. Roman-style archways were built on the courtyard side, while Greek-style colonnades without archways were built on the garden side. For greater comfort, Napoleon I had the peristyle enclosed with glass windows, making it into a vestibule entrance. The photograph shows the wing containing a long gallery, decorated with paintings by Jean Cotelle. These paintings depict the Versailles gardens as they were in Louis XIV's time. The gallery leads to the Garden Drawing Room, and, from there, a stone staircase with magnificent gilded-iron ramps, created during Louis XVI's reign, gives access to the Upper Parterre.
♦ 73

93 THE RIGHT WING OF THE GRAND TRIANON
♦ 73

AUTUMN

94 "THE CROSSROADS OF THE PHILOSOPHERS" → Map
Situated in the northwest corner of the North Parterre. The following terms were commissioned to decorate it: Apollonius by Mélo, Isocrates by Granier, Lysias by Dedieu, Theophrastes by Hurtrelle and Ulysses by Magnier. Strangely enough, Rayol's Plato and Lespagnandelle's Diogenes were placed on the Latona Half-Moon.
♦ 156-157-158-159

95 THE FOUNTAIN OF BACCHUS 261
This is the third Fountain of the Seasons, created in lead by Balthazar and Gaspard Marsy between 1673 and 1675, after a drawing by Charles Le Brun.
In the centre of an octagonal pool, Bacchus, representing Autumn, reclines with his head slightly turned. It seems as if his mysterious smile may have been borrowed from Leonardo da Vinci. The heavy grape clusters in his hands are suggestive of drunkenness.
Four little satyrs beside him, indulging in the pleasures of wine, form an indolent circle around the god.
♦ 42-57-70-110-144-173-176-179-184

96 NORTH QUINCUNX → Map
Term of Liberality
♦ 55

97 SOUTH QUINCUNX → Map
Term of Pomona
♦ 55

98 THE QUINCUNXES → Map
99 ♦ 55

100 PAETUS AND ARRIA 81
Group by François Lespingola (1644-1705) at the entrance of the Royal Avenue. In the 17th century it was thought that this group represented Paetus and his wife Arria. Paetus was condemned to death by the Emperor Claudius, whereupon his wife, Arria, set an example by stabbing herself and giving him the dagger. The group, however, is now believed to represent a gaul and his wife (see "The Dying Gladiator", p. 285, below).
Originally, the area in front of Louis XIII's hunting lodge was covered with woods. As time went on, the King had his master-gardeners, Jacques de Menours and Jacques Boyceau de la Barauderie, gradually landscape this area. They designed a square embroidered parterre around a circular pool. From there began a long, steeply sloping avenue that ended at the Fountain of the Swans. Later on, these square beds were replaced by two rectangular ones ending at a pool surrounded by two planted half-moon parterres. To the west, a narrowing walk (a visual effect popular during the Renaissance) led to the Fountain of the Swans, later to become the Fountain of Apollo.
Le Nôtre began altering this site in 1663. One major problem was the difference in level between the Fountain of the Swans and the parterre (94 feet). He cleverly handled this by designing broken-flight staircases and gentle, rounded slopes to surround the Parterre of Latona. In 1665, Bernini stopped at Versailles and saw the work in progress: the long avenue leading to the Fountain of the Swans was being widened. Two years later, as it was still rather narrow, it was enlarged to its present width with a half-moon at the entrance to the Latona Parterre. In 1680, a lawn carpet was placed in the centre of this avenue, hence its name, the Green Carpet.
A sculpted decorative arrangement of alternating white marble statues and vases was placed there, and in 1683 the Green Carpet became the Royal Avenue.
♦ 161

101 LAOCOON AND HIS SONS 82
This group is a marble copy by Jean-Baptiste Tubi (1635-1700) of a cast of a famous classical work kept at that time at the Royal Academy of Painting and Sculpture. The classical original was discovered in Rome in 1506 and was placed in the Belvedere at the Vatican Museum after its acquisition by Pope Julius II. Tubi's copy was made between 1678 and 1680. The French were already familiar with this group, as François I had already had a cast made of it.
The Laocoön in the Vatican was found in the ruins of Titus' palace and had suffered the effects of time. The right arms were mutilated

The Seasons

and were redone by Michelangelo. Recently a part of Laocoön's original right forearm was found and it was actually raised and bent at the elbow. In order to put it back on, the arm redone by Michelangelo had to be removed. The Versailles copy, however, has not been modified accordingly.

Stylistically speaking, the original dates from the Greek Hellenistic period. Pliny mentions the names of the sculptors: : Agesander, Polydorus and Athenodorus.

The story is rather tragic. Laocoön, high priest of Apollo in Troy, incurred his god's wrath when he committed a sacrilege. While he was preparing to make a sacrifice to the god Neptune, two immense serpents came out of the sea and wound round his sons. He ran to their aid but all three were strangled in the serpents' coils. This group was admired for its anatomical realism and variety of expression. Its influence on Michelangelo's work is undeniable.

The group by Tubi was first placed in the Trianon gardens facing the stairs to the Trianon-sous-Bois. During the Revolution it was brought to the entrance of the Royal Avenue, replacing "Perseus freeing Andromeda" by Puget, which was later moved to the Louvre.
Height: 4'3".
♦ 100

102 ARISTAEUS AND PROTEUS   136
Van Clève (1645-1735) was commissioned to make this group after a drawing by Girardon, but because of his demands, it was given over to Sébastien Slodtz (1655-1726). It bears his signature: "S. Slodtz natif d'Anvers 1723." (S. Slodtz, native of Antwerp, 1723).

Commissioned in 1688, it took 35 years to complete, longer than any other of the Versailles sculptures.

According to legend, Proteus, a sea deity, had the power of divination, but was so bad-tempered that one had to catch him while he was asleep and tie him up to prevent his escape. Aristaeus, Apollo's son, who needed Proteus' advice, is shown by Slodtz binding the god during his slumber.
Height: 7,6".
♦ 100

103 INO AND MELICERTES   135
Ino, wife of the Beotian king Athamas, had two sons, Learchus and Melicertes. She agreed to raise the young Bacchus (son of Jupiter and the mortal, Semele) as one of her own. Juno, who had been ridiculed by Jupiter, took revenge by making Ino and Athamas insane. Ino and Melicertes threw themselves into the sea. Venus, remembering that Ino was her granddaughter, called on Neptune for help. He agreed to give them the status of sea deities. Ino became Leucothea, and Melicertes, Palaemon.

Pierre Granier (1635-1715) depicts the mad Ino, with her son in her arms, throwing herself off a cliff. The marble group was carved between 1686 and 1691 after a model by Girardon.
Height: 9'10".
♦ 100

104 THE FOUNTAIN OF ENCELADUS   →
105 The Giant, Enceladus, in the centre of the pool, lies "crushed under the mountain of rocks he had built up to the sky."   Map

The expression of pain and horror is striking. "The head is especially beautiful; so much in the style of Jules Romain that this great man could not disclaim the drawing if he were alive."

The once-gilded, sculpted lead work was executed by Gaspard Marsy (1629-1681) in 1676. Originally, eight basins spouting water surrounded the central pool, and the grove was decorated with a floral trellis structure topped with flower pots.
♦ 133-151

106 THE TEMPLE OF LOVE
This pavilion, of a very pure architectural style, was erected in 1778, at the same time as the Belvedere, by Richard Mique, formerly architect to King Stanislas Leszczynski and his daughter, Queen Marie, wife of Louis XV.

The temple was set on an artificial "island" between two arms of the "river." It is a rotunda similar to the Temple of Vesta in Rome, composed of twelve Corinthian columns surmounted by a cupola in Conflans stone. A large, carved trophy of cupid's attributes with flowers stands in the centre. The floor is in white marble with red edging. The sculptor, Deschamps, gave Marie-Antoinette a wax model of this building. It was decided to place the statue of Cupid carved by Bouchardon in the temple. It is now in the Louvre, but was replaced by a copy made by the same sculptor for Madame de Pompadour. The bridges leading to the temple were decorated with flowers like dame's violets and gillyflowers. Paradise apple trees were planted around the Temple on the island.

Marie-Antoinette could take in this delightful view from her bedchamber in the Petit Trianon. Although entirely artificial, it conformed to the then-popular theories about "returning to nature," advocated by Jean-Jacques Rousseau.
♦ 65

107 VENUS RISING FROM THE SEA   120
One of the most exquisite statues at Versailles, created between 1685 and 1696. It was inspired by a classical original in Cardinal de Richelieu's collection which was kept in his château. Although it was admired by some of the most discriminating 17th century connoisseurs, like Poussin and Bernini, it has since completely disappeared.

This Venus, the torso of which is copied from a lost classical model, was begun by Sarrazin, continued by Le Hongre and finally completed by Pierre Le Gros (1629-1714), to whom it is usually attributed.
White marble. Height: 7'3".
♦ 100

108 THE FISHERY,
OR THE "MARLBOROUGH TOWER"
In 1783, when Richard Mique began construction of Marie-Antoinette's Hamlet, "The Duke of Marlborough was in vogue." The song written in 1722 at the death of the famous English general was revived by Beaumarchais in "The Marriage of Figaro." Although the play had been immediately censored, the Queen would have it put on in her little Trianon theatre. It was said that the King and the Queen heard the Dauphin's nurse singing the tune and asked her to teach it to them.

The Seasons

Marlborough became a fashionable hero and Marie-Antoinette felt that she had to have a tower named after him in her hamlet.
The tower, as well as the adjoining Dairy and other cottages, were painted to imitate old brick and crumbling stone. The work was done by the painters Tolède and Dardignac. People were able to fish in the lake directly from the tower. The lake was fed by the Trèfle reservoir and stocked with 2349 carp and 26 pikes.

109 THE BELVEDERE
Trees border the ponds which run from the Belvedere to Marie-Antoinette's Hamlet. In autumn, these trees, some of them centuries old, shade the winding banks with a tawny canopy of leaves mixed with the golden hues of chestnut trees.
♦ 65-106-108

WINTER

110 THE FOUNTAIN OF SATURN 272
Three years after creating this pool, François Girardon executed the marble statue of the same subject using the same theme. The Fountain of Winter was the last one to be completed; the work was executed between 1673 and 1675. The sculptor followed the model by Le Brun, who himself had used an iconography of winter developed by Poussin. It was Poussin who had chosen Saturn. The winged god is seated on the island, holding a sack containing the stone Cybele had substituted for Jupiter. Surrounding him are four children with winter's attributes; one holds a mask, another a bellows.
♦ 42-57-70-95-179

111 THE FOUNTAIN OF LATONA 72
AND THE LIZARD FOUNTAINS 73
During the reign of Louis XIII, the parterre in front of the château led to a steep slope ending at what was to become the Green Carpet or Royal Avenue. In 1668 Le Nôtre completely altered this section by digging out the area to accommodate the Parterre of Latona; it could be reached by a large staircase or two elegantly-designed slopes.
A large circular pool was placed in the middle of the parterre, with the famous marble group carved by Gaspard and Balthazar Marsy in the centre, on a platform. The group was executed between 1668 and 1671. Around the central group stood six lead figures of Lycian peasants transformed into amphibians, and on the rim, twenty frogs spouting water.
Two round pools, the Lizard Fountains, each containing two other figures of peasants being transformed, were placed on either side of the central avenue of the parterre. No doubt influenced by Mansart, the King agreed to alter the height of the central group, setting it at the top of four pink and white marble superimposed basins. Thus, Latona and her children were elevated above the axis of the sun. We should remember that during the Fronde insurrection, Anne of Austria and her children were forced to flee on a winter night from Paris in order to escape the unrest...
Figures of Lycian peasants and frogs were placed on the various levels; the number of frogs was increased.
It should also be mentioned that Latona was originally facing east. She now faces west, arms raised, imploring Jupiter, while her children huddle against her in fright. Within reasonable limits, it could be said that, on a symbolic level, the Latona group is to the gardens what the King's Bedchamber is to the palace: the focal point.
♦ 193-194-195-224-225

112 THE SEINE BY LE HONGRE 26
Étienne Le Hongre portrayed the river Seine as a bearded man crowned with grapes and flowers leaning on an oar adorned with crayfish. The cornucopia symbolizes the abundance of the regions fertilized by the river. The clay model was paid for in 1687. The date of the casting is inscribed on the oar: *"Fondu par les Keller 1690"*. The statue sits on the west rim of the north pool.
♦ 24-25-124-230

113 WATER PARTERRE: NYMPHS 28
Philippe Magnier received 2,800 livres 29
between 1685 and 1687 for his models of the two nymphs side by side on the north pool. This crowned nymph leans on a shell and holds a map. Next to her, a cupid blows on a shell. On the edge of the map we read *"Phil Magnier F"* and on the shell, *"Fondv par les Keller 1689"*.
♦ 17-125-230-232-234

114 GANYMEDE BY LAVIRON 56
AND THE NORTH LATONA SLOPE
♦ 63-141

115 WINTER BY GIRARDON 218
THE NORTH PARTERRE
♦ 27-42-110-131

116 THE WATER PARTERRE: 15
CHILDREN WITH A MIRROR
There are two groups depicting this theme on the north rim of the south pool. This one was begun by Pierre Laviron in 1686 and the clay model completed by Pierre Legros. The three children carry a garland of flowers, but one of them seems to be seated and holds a mirror in his raised left hand.
♦ 122-252-255-256

117 THE KNIFE-GRINDER, OR L'ARROTINO 232
The white marble statue of the Knife-Grinder, which was copied in 1684 by Foggini (1652-1725) for this site, was taken to the Tuileries in 1871. It was replaced by this bronze, cast by the Kellers in 1688. Its position on the steps of the North Parterre is symmetrically related to that of the Kneeling Venus by Coysevox.
The Hellenistic model of the Knife-Grinder, also called "L'Arrotino," was acquired by Duke Cosimo de Medici in 1578 and in 1688 was

The Seasons

placed in the famous "Tribuna" of the Uffizi Palace in Florence. It is the only existing copy of an original from the Pergamum School. Some art historians think that it might actually be the original.
Bronze. Height: 3'5".
♦ 145

118 FOUNTAIN OF DAYBREAK — 35
119 In 1684, construction began on two of the "Fountains of Animal Combat," which are part of the Water Parterre and flank the steps leading down to the Parterre of Latona. These two raised pools were completed in 1687.
On each side of the frontal rim sit two fighting animals cast by the Kellers.
To the north is the Fountain of Diana, named after the marble statue by Desjardins. On the rim a lion brings down a boar (by Jean Raon and Corneille Van Clève) and another lion brings down a wolf (same sculptors).
The second Fountain, to the south, is called "Daybreak," after the statue by Gaspard Marsy. On the rim, a tiger brings down a bear and a stag is killed by a bloodhound (models by Houzeau). The two Fountains come alive with a large central spray in the main pool. The victorious animals spout water towards the main spray, while the defeated spew water towards the lower pools.
♦ 28-30-32-36-38-39-40-45-130-132-150

120 THE SAONE BY TUBI — 14
The bronze statues emerge from the snow-covered expanse. A few water droplets are all that is left of the night's snowfall; they form beads on the dark surface of the statuary in the morning sun.
♦ 237

121 THE WATER PARTERRE: — 9
GROUP OF CHILDREN
Between 1685 and 1687, François Lespingola and Jacques Buirette were paid for two groups of three children which were placed on the Water Parterre.
They hold a garland of flowers and one kneels on a dolphin.
♦ 123-252-255

122 THE WATER PARTERRE: — 18
CHILDREN WITH A MIRROR
In 1687, Jean Poulletier received 1,000 livres for his clay model. Aubry and Roger were paid for the cast in 1690. A child looks at himself in a mirror, a cupid carries a bow, and the last figure, seated on a dolphin, holds a garland of flowers.
♦ 116-121-252-255-256

123 GROUP OF CHILDREN — 15
FROM THE WATER PARTERRE
BY LAVIRON AND LE GROS
The same group as the one in the photograph on page 116 seen here in a rare winter setting.
♦ 116-121-252-253-255-256

124 THE SEINE BY LE HONGRE — 26
♦ 24-25-112-230

125 NYMPH WITH A GARLAND — 22
BY LE GROS
♦ 17-230-232-234

126 THE COLONNADE — 273
127 The Colonnade was built in late 1684 on the site of the former Grove of the Springs by Mansart and Le Nôtre. It is a 104-foot diameter rotunda punctuated by 32 columns in different marbles, supporting bas-relief archways, counterbalanced by 32 marble pilasters. The idea was to show that marble was "presently more common in France than in Italy." Between the columns, twenty-eight magnificent basins in white marble spew high sprays of water. It is impossible to cite the names of all those who carved the vases, spandrels and fountains; virtually the entire team at Versailles was involved.
In 1699, Louis XIV decided to have the "Rape of Persephone by Pluto" placed in the centre of the colonnade, and it remained there until recently. It was removed to protect it from the weather.
♦ 27

128 BRONZE VASE, SOUTH PARTERRE — → Map
The vase is decorated with garlands of grape leaves. Young smiling satyrs looking at one another form the handles.
♦ 22-23-76-77-129-162-248-249

129 BRONZE VASE, SOUTH PARTERRE — → Map
Sphinxes form the handles of this vase. They lean against the edge of the urn and rest their claws on lions' heads.
♦ 22-23-71-76-77-128-162-248-249

130 AIR BY LE HONGRE — 31
♦ 27-28

131 WINTER — 105
This white marble term stands in the North Quincunx. It has been difficult to identify the sculptor due to lack of documents. First it was attributed to Théodon, who received instructions in Rome in 1679 to complete the Winter and Spring terms.
Since then, similarities in style have been noted in four marble terms from Saint-Cloud kept in the Louvre. One of these, called "Winter," is close in style to the one in the Quincunxes, and is attributed to Pierre Le Gros.
♦ 42-55-110

133 THE FOUNTAIN OF ENCELADUS
BY GASPARD MARSY
♦ 104-105-151

134 THE GROVE OF THE DOMES
Formerly called the Grove of Fame (1675) after the lead statue with a large spray of water in the centre of the pool. In 1684, Louis XIV ordered the removal of the figure, which was damaged, "wishing to do something magnificent in this spot." The groups from the Grotto of Tethys were brought here, as well as Acis and Galatea, and were placed between the white marble pavilions built by Mansart between 1677 and 1678, and adorned with bronze trophies.
New sculptures were then commissioned: Daybreak by Le Gros, Arion by Jean Raon, Ino by Rayol, and Diana by René Frémin. The grove was then given the name of Apollo's Baths, and it contained the exquisite Amphitrite by Anguier.

The Assembly of Olympus

But in 1699 the King asked to have the main figures from the Grotto of Tethys protected under dome-shaped canopies supported by iron columns.

Finally, in 1704, he had these groups transferred to the Marsh Grove. This same year, Dawn by Magnier and the Nymph by Anselme Flamen came to the Grove of the Domes.

During the reign of Louis XVIII the marble pavilions were falling to ruin and had to be razed.
♦ 135-198-200

135 DAWN
Philippe Magnier chose to represent Dawn as Flora, using a drawing by Girardon. The statue, begun in 1686, was placed in the Grove of the Domes in 1704. During the 19th century, it met with the same fate as the other statues in the Grove.
♦ 44-57-62-134-198-200

THE ASSEMBLY OF OLYMPUS

136 THE APOTHEOSIS OF HERCULES
137 The idea for this drawing room, later called "The Hercules Drawing Room," dates back to the time of Louis XIV, when the old chapel located on this site was destroyed. It lies at the junction of the North Wing and the State Apartment in the central section. It was decided to display here the magnificent painting given to Louis XIV by the Venetian Republic in 1664, "Feast in the House of Simon" by Paolo Caliari, known as Veronese. Facing this enormous masterpiece, above the fireplace, is "Eliezer and Rebecca," also by Veronese. Sold to the King by Mazarin's heirs, this work came from the famous banker-collector Jabach.

Work was interrupted at the death of Louis XIV, but resumed in 1724 for the marble work. In 1733, François Lemoine was asked to paint the Apotheosis of Hercules on the vaulted ceiling. It was an appropriate allegory for showing how "the love of Virtue raises Man above himself and makes him superior to the most difficult and perilous tasks. Obstacles vanish when the interests of the King and the nation are concerned; assisted by honour and guided by fidelity, he attains immortality through his actions." (Lépicié).

The subject was fascinating, but the difficulty lay in expressing it visually; next to Veronese's two masterpieces it would certainly be subjected to comparison. There were also the two magnificent ceilings by Charles Le Brun in the nearby State Apartment and the Hall of Mirrors.

Lemoine accepted the challenge. In 1736 when Voltaire saw the ceiling, he exclaimed: "Nowhere in Europe is there a painting as immense as Le Moyne's ceiling, and I doubt if there is a more beautiful one."

The painter refused to use Le Brun's system of a "compartmented" ceiling, but succeeded in harmonizing his work with that of Veronese. The eye immediately goes to the focal point of the work: Hercules' ascension to Olympus where an assembly of gods awaits him. The hero, whose chariot is pulled by "the Spirits of Virtue," holds his famous club. Jupiter and Juno are waiting for him, and the king of the gods holds the beautiful Hebe by the hand, crowned with flowers, and presents her to Hercules. Slightly below, on the left, Bacchus is leaning on his elbows, daydreaming; next is a naked Venus, being crowned with flowers by the Graces. Under Jupiter's eagle, Diana with her bow "tells Pandora of her thoughts." In the upper left hand corner, Mercury, holding his caduceus, watches the extraordinary event below: man deified.
♦ 146-171-174

138 NYMPH WITH A SHELL
The original, mentioned in the Borghese collections as early as 1638, is a classical work dating from the 2nd century B.C. Napoleon I bought it from his brother-in-law Camillo Borghese, husband to the lovely Pauline; he also bought the rest of the former's collection (now in the Louvre).

This work was highly valued throughout the 17th century, which explains why Coysevox was commissioned (1683-1685) to make a copy of it. His copy is far superior to the original. The French work was still appreciated during the following century. Indeed, it was taken to the Louvre in 1891 and replaced by the present statue carved by Suchetet.

139 THE APOLLO BELVEDERE
The original is a classical statue attributed to the Greek, Leochares, around 330 B.C. The copy in the Vatican dates from 130 A.D.

This Apollo was discovered in the gardens of Cardinal della Rovere, the future Pope Julius II. He had it taken to the Vatican in 1509, and placed in the Belvedere courtyard in 1511.

It was regarded as one of the finest achievements of Greek art and renowned the world over. Several copies were made, such as the one for François I, who wanted a cast of it for Fontainebleau. It is quite obvious the influence this work had on the sculptors of the classical Versailles period. Girardon's famous group in the Grotto of Tethys is proof of this.

The copy found on the south slope of the Fountain of Latona was created by Pierre Mazeline (1632-1708) in 1682. We should mention that at this time copies were as highly considered as originals.
♦ 144-202

140 JUPITER
This white marble term was carved by Jean-Jacques Clérion (1637-1714), from 1686 to 1687, at the same time as the term of Juno. The god holds a thunderbolt in his right hand, like Mignard's model.
Height: 8'10".

141 GANYMEDE
♦ 63-114

The Assembly of Olympus

142 MERCURY
This white marble term was carved between 1684 and 1697 by Corneille Van Clève (1645-1735).
The god of merchants holds a purse in his right hand and wears his famous winged hat.
Height: approximately 9 feet.

143 PANDORA
White marble term carved by Pierre Legros (1629-1714) after a drawing by Mignard.
Height: 9'2".

144 BACCHUS
The great bronze period at Versailles began in 1684; this noble element was considered imperishable. The first statues to be cast were of Bacchus, Apollo, Hermes and Silenus (between 1684 and 1685); next came the children in the Water Avenue, the Venus and the Knife-Grinder for the North Parterre originally meant for Marly, and finally the admirable ensemble for the Water Parterre.
All of these works could not have been so well-executed so rapidly had it not been for the help of two skilled craftsmen from Zurich: Jean-Jacques and Jean-Balthasar Keller. They had originally been summoned to fabricate artillery parts at the Paris Arsenal!
According to records, in 1691 and 1701 the four bronzes near the château façade were originally placed on the steps of the South Parterre, near the Orangery.
The Bacchus was copied from the "Richelieu Bacchus," a classical work in the royal collections now in the Louvre. Its rather smooth lines are evidence of an exaggerated Praxitelean tendency.
The Apollo Belvedere and the Mercury are copies of classical statues in the Vatican museum. The statue of Silenus carrying young Bacchus comes from the Prince Borghese Collection purchased by Napoleon I for the Louvre. A replica commissioned for the Marly gardens is also in the Louvre. The fact that these four figures were carved in marble as well as being cast in bronze for the Versailles gardens is proof of the importance ascribed to these works in the 17th century.
Bronze. Height: approximately 6'6".

145 THE KNEELING VENUS
This bronze statue was cast by the Keller brothers in 1696 from a marble carved ten years earlier by Antoine Coysevox (1640-1720).
Originally, and until 1871, the Coysevox marble, an imitation of a famous Greek original, adorned the steps of the North Parterrre. In 1871, it was sent to the Tuileries and in 1873, to the Louvre. To replace it, Versailles recovered the Keller cast originally made for the Tuileries but placed in the Marly gardens until the Revolution (1789). The bronze was then sent to the Tuileries and remained there until 1871, when it came to Versailles.
It was assumed that the classical marble was by Phidias, and Coysevox inscribed Phidias' name on the marble as well as his own. But it was actually Doidalces of Bithynia who sculpted the original. He became known for having created a Kneeling Aphrodite on display in Rome in the Porticus of Octavia.
There is a fine copy of this statue (mid 3rd century B.C.), in the Louvre since 1879. It was discovered near Vienne, France.
Many art lovers admire Coysevox's work, considering it to be superior to its original.
Bronze. Height: 5'11".
♦ 37-107-148

146 HERCULES
This white marble statue was executed between 1684 and 1685 by Noël Jouvenet, who died in 1716. It was created after a plaster cast (1683) of a Greek sculpture in the classical statue reserve, now in the Chiaramonti Museum (Vatican). The work in the Vatican is itself a reproduction of a missing original of the 4th century B.C. The model is actually Emperor Commodus (161-192 A.D.), son of Marcus Aurelius, unfortunately known for his great cruelty. He is depicted as Hercules, holding the young Telephus in one arm and his club in the other. The skin of the lion of Nemea is knotted around his shoulders.
Height: 4'1".

147 VENUS
Carved by Nicolas Frémery (died after 1687), it is an exact replica of one of the most famous classical statues. Like Octavius, now in the Louvre, and once in the Hall of Mirrors, it is signed "Cleomenes." This statue was placed in the "Tribuna" of the Uffizi Museum in Florence in 1688. It was taken from a prototype by Praxiteles of the 3rd century B.C.
Louis XIV commissioned Carlier, Clérion, Coysevox and Frémery to do at least five replicas of the original.
The work pictured here was begun by the sculptor Michel Mosnier and, after his death, was completed by Frémery. At his feet lie a dolphin and two small cupids. The presence of this statue on the Green Carpet of the Royal Avenue should remind us that in the 1st century, Julius Caesar, who belonged to the gens Julia, considered himself a descendant of Aeneas, son of Venus, and therefore divine himself.
White marble. Height: approximately 5'6".

148 THE CALLIPYGEAN VENUS
The classical original is mentioned from 1594 onwards as part of the collections in the Farnese Palace in Rome (now the French Embassy). Taken to Naples in 1786, it was placed in the National Museum there in 1802. The copy by Jean-Jacques Clérion (1637-1714) was made for Versailles between 1684 and 1686, while the second copy was done by François Barois for the Marly gardens (today in the Louvre).
Height: over 6'6".

149 FAUN IN THE MIST
In a corner of the north slope of the Parterre of Latona. This faun is placed symmetrically in relation to the Callipygean Venus on the south slope.
♦ 58

150 THE FOUNTAIN OF DIANA
♦ 118-132

The presence of Antiquity

151 THE FOUNTAIN OF ENCELADUS
♦ 104-133

THE PRESENCE OF ANTIQUITY

152 ARTEMESIA — 116
Begun by the sculptor A. Lefèvre in 1687 and completed by Martin Desjardins (1637-1694) in the year of his death.
Placed among the classical vases and statues on the Green Carpet, Artemesia, as well as Cunning, Achilles and Dido, stands out because of its modern and almost romantic style.
The Queen is about to drink the brew containing the ashes of her husband, King Mausolus.
White marble. Height: about 6'6".
♦ 100

153 DIDO ON THE WOODPILE — 124
This work by Jean Poulletier (1653-1719), moving in its passion and suffering, is first mentioned in 1694; it must therefore have been completed by this date.
On the Green Carpet, this Dido, owing to its candour, contrasts even more than Achilles and Artemesia with the classically-inspired statues.
White marble. Height: 7'5".
♦ 100-152-155

154 CYPARISSUS AND HIS DEER — 115
This group was made by Anselme Flamen (1647-1717) between 1687 and 1688, probably after a model by Girardon. Cyparissus, known for his beauty and loved by Apollo, caresses his beloved deer that he is later to kill by accident.
White marble. Height: about 6'6".
♦ 100

155 AMAZON — 127
Created between 1685 and 1693 by Jacques Buirette (1631-1699) after a cast of the classical work in the Capitoline Museum, with certain variations.
Another classical replica is in the Vatican Museum; we know it was highly valued by the Emperor Augustus.
White marble. Height: about 6'6".

155 ACHILLES AT SCYROS — 128
A work both particularly original in its conception and in its romantic spirit; it is signed and dated "Philb. Vigier Molinensis 1695."
Legend has it that during the Trojan War, Thetis wished to keep her son Achilles safe from the Greeks. She decided to hide him in the home of the King of Scyros with his daughters. Ulysses went to the King's home and offered his daughters jewels and weapons as gifts. The Princesses chose the jewels, but Achilles, although dressed as they were, gave himself away by taking the weapons.
This explains Vigier's portrayal. Achilles, wearing a dress, unsheathes his sword.
Open jewellery boxes lie at his feet.
White marble. Height: more than 6'6".

156 LYSIAS — 213
The terms placed on the North Parterre at the "Crossroads of the Philosophers" mark the "downfall" of Le Brun after the death of Colbert: they were based on drawings by his arch rival, Pierre Mignard, later to became First Painter to the King.
Lysias (about 440-380 B.C.) was a famous Athenian orator. Jean Dedieu (1646-1726) depicted a bearded old man holding a parchment roll in his left hand (1685).
Height: 9'5".
♦ 94

156 THEOPHRASTUS — 212
This white marble term was carved by Simon Hurtrelle (1684-1724) between 1686 and 1688, after drawings by Mignard.
Theophrastus, Greek philosopher and author of "Characters," is dressed in a robe with his head covered. "The inverted poppies he holds show that he was an enemy of sleep." (Piganiol).
Height: 8'11".
♦ 94

157 ISOCRATES — 211
This white marble term was carved by Pierre Granier (1635-1715) between 1685 and 1688, after Mignard.
The famous Athenian orator (436-338 B.C.) wears a cloak covering his head. He holds a rolled parchment in his left hand and in his right, a sheet of paper, reminder of his eloquent speeches and addresses.
Height: 9'5".
♦ 94

157 APOLLONIUS — 214
White marble term by Barthélémy de Mélo, after Mignard, carved between 1685 and 1687.
It may be a representation of Apollonius of Rhodes (3rd century B.C.), a poet from Alexandria and eloquent and ingenious author of the "Argonautica." The sheet of paper he holds in his right hand suggests this. This statue may also be the philosopher Apollonius, tutor to Marcus Aurelius, in the company of other "sages of antiquity."
Height: about 9'5".
♦ 94

158 CIRCE — 75
The famous magician in the "Odyssey", who used all manner of spells to keep Ulysses and his companions on her island. She is crowned with flowers and leaves and holds a wand in her right hand.
This work was carved in 1684 by Laurent Magnier, known as the "Roman" (about 1619-1700).
Height: about 9'1".

158 PLATO — 76
White marble term by Joseph Rayol (1655-1718), executed between 1686 and 1688.
Plato (429-347 B.C.), the author of the "Sym-

posium," searches for truth in "ideas." He was a disciple of Socrates and a teacher of Aristotle. He is depicted here with a tongue of fire on his brow, like an apostle on the day of the Pentecost, holding a medallion representing Socrates.
Height: about 9'1".

159 ULYSSES — 210
White marble term by Philippe Magnier (1647-1715), carved between 1684 and 1688 after a drawing by Mignard.
The hero of Homer's "Odyssey" holds the plant Mercury gave him to protect him from Circe's spells. This plant gave him power and Circe agreed to befriend him. She had transformed his companions into swine, but restored them to their human form.
Height: about 9'5".
♦ 94

159 DIOGENES — 87
White marble term by Mathieu Lespagnandelle (1616-1689), carved between 1685 and 1688 after a drawing by Mignard.
Diogenes the Cynic (413-323 B.C.) scorned all conventions and lived on nothing. When asked by Alexander the Great if he wanted anything, he replied, "Yes, for you to get out of my light!". This insolence is not apparent in the Versailles version. He is merely holding a parchment in his hand.
Height: 9'5".

160 THE FARNESE CAPTIVES — 50
OR BARBARIAN PRISONERS — 41
The first statue, situated on the north slope of the Parterre of Latona, was carved by Antoine André, known as "the Roman," between 1684 and 1687. The second figure, placed symmetrically with the first on the south slope of the Parterre of Latona, was carved at the same time by Mathieu Lespagnandelle.
They are marble copies of the "Farnese Captives," discovered in Rome in Trajan's Forum and displayed since 1819 in the Naples National Museum. Identifying them has been difficult; they have been referred to as the Kings of Armenia, the Kings of the Dacians, Slave Kings, etc. The Versailles copies were created from plaster casts kept in the royal collections.
Height: 7'5".

161 THE DYING GLADIATOR — 74
This white marble copy was made by Michel Mosnier (or Monnier) in 1685 after a classical work in the Ludovisi Collection which was bought by Pope Clément II in 1737 and, since that time, it has been on display in the Capitoline Museum in Rome. This classical statue, as well as the group "Paetus and Arria", was probably a replica of a work by Epigonus intended for Attalus I's ex-voto monument in Pergamum. This offering celebrated Attalus' victory over the Gauls in about 230 B.C.

161 PAETUS AND ARRIA — 81
This statue in white marble by François Lespingola (1644-1705), created between 1684 and 1688, is a copy after a plaster cast in the royal collections. The original classical group was first in the old Ludovisi collection, but has been on display since 1901 in the Baths of the National Museum in Rome. It was entitled "Paetus and Arria" in the 17th century, but is now believed to represent a Gaul and his wife, figures from the Attalus I monument (see "The Dying Gladiator" above).
Lespingola carefully sculpted the woman's hair, which had been roughly done in the classical model.
This group used to stand at the end of the Parterre of Latona but was transferred to the entrance of the Green Carpet after the Milo of Crotone was taken to the Louvre in 1820.
Height: about 7'4".
♦ 100

FROM WAR TO PEACE

162 BRONZE VASES WITH APOLLONIAN MOTIFS: → Map
SOUTH PARTERRE
One of the bronze vases in the South Parterre. Dragons form the handles. On one side of the vase Apollo slays the terrifying Python with his arrows.
On the other side is depicted an episode from the Apollo legend in which the nymph Daphne is transformed into a laurel tree.
♦ 22-23-76-77-128-129-248-249

163 FIGURES ON THE DRAGON FOUNTAIN → Map
164 (DETAIL)
165 Before the construction of the Fountain of Neptune (begun in 1679), the view of the Water Avenue ended at the Dragon Fountain. This fountain, enlarged in the 18th century, was completely redone for the 1789 centennial festivities. It then measured 130 feet in diameter, and using fragments of the remaining sculptures, Tony Noël redid all of the lead decoration. All that remains of Gaspard and Balthasar Marsy's work is the restored dragon. The original included a dragon (spouting water up to 87 feet), four dolphins, and four children riding swans.

166 THE HALL OF MIRRORS
167 "Nothing equals the beauty of the Hall of Mirrors. This type of majesty is unique in the world." (Marie de Rabutin-Chantal, marquise de Sévigné).
The work schedule for the Hall was presented to Louis XIV by Jules Hardouin-Mansart on September 26, 1678. The Hall and the War and Peace Drawing Rooms run along the entire west façade of the central section, on the former site of the King's Pavilion, the terrace and the Queen's Pavilion, all built by Le Vau. The decoration was carried out under the supervision of Charles Le Brun, and was completed in 1686. The dimensions of the structure, the luxurious materials and magnificent vaulted ceiling, all glorify the divine-right monarchy which was

From War to Peace

later to became an absolute monarchy under Louis XIV.

The ceiling painted by Charles Le Brun depicts the first seventeen years of Louis XIV's "personal reign," which began in 1661 at the death of Cardinal Mazarin, Prime Minister, godfather and perhaps stepfather to the young king. There are seventeen arched windows and, facing them, the same number of "glass mirror" arcades, manufactured in the Saint-Gobain workshops. Never before had so many mirrors of such size been seen anywhere. Arcades and windows are separated by Rance marble pilasters which sit on green campana pedestals bordered in white veined marble. The finest classical statues in the royal collections were placed in the four central niches and on either side of the entrances to the War and Peace Drawing Rooms. Four of the eight statues, "The Modest Venus," "Modesty," "Urania" and the "Versailles Bacchus," have been returned to their original places. The "Vestal Virgin," the famous "Germanicus," "Augustus" by Cleomenes and "Diana with a Doe" are now in the Louvre, as well as the "Arles Venus," restored by Girardon for the Hall.

Although we cannot name every sculptor who carved the trophies on the ceiling cornice where the vault begins, we shall mention Coysevox, Clérion, Le Gros, Lecomte, Massou and Flamen.

This dazzling setting was decorated with silver furniture which Louis XIV later had melted down in 1689. Here the King held "state audiences" for the Doge of Genoa in 1685, the ambassadors of the King of Siam in 1686, the Persian ambassadors in 1715, and the ambassador of the Ottoman Empire in 1742. Receptions and games were held here in honour of royal marriages, but rarely balls. Here on January 3, 1805, Pope Pius VII blessed the crowds which had poured into the gardens. Here on January 18, 1871, the German Empire was born, although it meant disaster for France. Bismarck, the Prussian chancellor, proclaimed his king as Emperor of all German kings. Finally, on June 28, 1919, after four years of suffering and bloodshed, the treaty ending the First World War was signed. The present-day furnishings, particularly the candlestands with figures of women and children (models by Babel, Gondouin and Foliot), are replicas of the furniture ordered by Louis XV for the festivities honouring the marriage of the Dauphin to Marie-Antoinette, Archduchess of Austria, on May 16, 1770.

168 THE WAR VASE — 6

The War and Peace Vases stand at either end of the terrace in front of the Hall of Mirrors, overlooking the Water Parterre. The theme of Louis XIV's triumphs, depicted by Charles Le Brun on the painted ceilings, is also portrayed outside the château on these vases. The War Vase, on the north west corner of the slope, was carved by Antoine Coysevox between 1684 and 1685. Satyr-head handles are attached to a belly adorned with broad acanthus leaves. Above, the body is decorated with a bas-relief depicting France as Minerva with a docile lion, accepting tribute from Spain. The other side shows Hercules pursuing the fleeing Turks. This scene is an allusion to the aid His Most Holy King sent to the Emperor in the war against the Turks in Hungary.

Height: approximately 8 feet.

169 THE PEACE VASE — 5

The creation of this vase was entrusted to Jean-Baptiste Tubi in 1684. A sculptor of Italian origin, Tubi was born in Rome and became a French citizen in 1672. This work evokes the Treaty of Nijmegen, in which Spain made concessions, marking the pinnacle of Louis XIV's power. In a frieze similar to Phidias' "Panathenea," Tubi's flowing style depicts a procession of Fame figures bringing olive branches to the King seated under a tree. Obeying the order to cease combat, Hercules has thrown down his club and stands calmly before him.

Height: approximately 8 feet.

170 ACHELOUS — 79

Bearing the same name as the largest river in Greece, the son of Oceanus and Tethys is considered the oldest of the three thousand river gods, all brothers. He is also the source of many legends, such as those linked to the Hercules cycle.

The white marble term, signed and dated 1688, was carved after a model by Girardon. Simon Mazière depicts Achelous in his human form as a bearded man crowned with reeds, holding a cornucopia.

Height: over 8 feet.

171 HERCULES

The theme of Hercules, the man who achieved divinity through strength and courage, greatly inspired the artists at Versailles. We should remember that Le Brun originally considered this theme for the Hall of Mirrors.

We find it in this white marble term carved by Louis Le Comte (1650-1681) between 1684 and 1686. Clothed in the skin of the lion of Nemea, the hero carries his club on his shoulder and holds three apples from the Gardens of the Hesperides in his left hand.

Height: 9'1".

ABUNDANCE

172 VERTUMNUS AND POMONA — 131 / 140

These two white marble terms by Étienne Le Hongre (1628-1690), placed symmetrically on either side of the Green Carpet axis at the half-moon of the Fountain of Apollo, were created between 1684 and 1689 after Le Brun. According to mythology, these two gods are related to the earth's fertility and the four seasons. We can recognize Vertumnus, crowned with leaves and flowers, by the basket of fruit he carries; and

The Dionysian Current

173 BACCHUS — 132
The model for this term was begun by Jean Dugoulon; it was Jean Raon (1630-1707) however who carved it in marble between 1687 and 1693. Bacchus, god of wine and delirious excess, is depicted here in a rather conventional manner.
He holds a "thyrsus" entwined with grape branches in his left hand; he wears a crown of grape leaves and squeezes a bunch of grapes in his right hand. A lion's skin is draped around his waist.
Height: approx. 9'1".

Pomona, wearing a tiara, by the garland of flowers and fruit she holds.
Height: 9'5".

174 POMONA — 93
Term in the Quincunxes
♦ 55-59-74-131-175-176-177-182-183-185

175 HERCULES — 92
Term in the Quincunxes
♦ 55-59-74-131-175-176-177-182-183-185

175 LIBERALITY — 100
Term in the Quincunxes
♦ 55-59-74-131-174-176-177-182-183-185

176 BACCHUS — 103
Term in the Quincunxes
♦ 55-59-74-131-174-175-177-182-183-184-185

176 ABUNDANCE — 104
177 Term in the Quincunxes
♦ 55-59-74-131-174-175-176-182-183-185

THE DIONYSIAN CURRENT

178 BACCHANTE OR MAENAD — 85
White marble term carved by Jean Dedieu (1646-1727), between 1684 and 1685, at the same time as the Lysias term. While this bacchante, like the others, is partly-clothed in a lion's skin, she does not have the traditional thyrsus entwined with ivy and grape branches, but a tambourine, as a reminder that she too, like the Muses, inspires poets.
Height: 8'11".

179 FOUNTAIN OF BACCHUS — 215
♦ 57-70-95-110-184

180 SYRINX — 137
Syrinx is the nymph who jumped into Lake Ladon to escape Pan's attentions and then was turned into reeds. Pan then bound together with wax reeds of different lengths and made a flute which he called "Syrinx."
The hamadryad on this marble term, signed and dated "Simon Mazière 1689", carries a tuft of reeds.
Height: 9'1".

181 PAN — 134
The god so often confused with the satyrs and sileni is shown here with a syrinx, the shepherd's pipe he made from cut reeds.
When Simon Mazière carved Pan in 1687 (after Girardon?) he did not portray him with the legendary ugliness that so amused the gods that they gave him a name meaning "all." Since the god Pan is represented here as a term, the most unusual parts of his body, the goat's legs, are not shown.
Height: 9'1".

182 PAN — 99
Term in the Quincunxes
Carved by Domenico Guidi, after Poussin.
♦ 55-59-74-186

182 FAUN — 221
♦ 27-53

183 FAUN — 101
Carved by Domenico Guidi, after Poussin.
♦ 55-59-74

184 BACCHUS OR AUTUMN — 215
Thomas Regnaudin (1622-1706) was paid for the plaster model in 1680, but it was not until fourteen years later that he was finally paid for the marble statue. Bacchus, with a cup in his hand, is represented rather traditionally by the sculptor as the god of wine and drunkenness. Although the marble does not have the expressiveness of the Marsy Bacchus, it does bear the mark of Regnaudin's talent.
Height: 6'6".
♦ 27-42-95-173-176-179

185 BACCHANTE OR MAENAD — 95
Terms in the Quincunxes
♦ 55

186 PAN — 134
Term in the half-moon of the Fountain of Apollo
♦ 180-181-182

186 CHILD WITH GRAPES — 201
This child playing with a cluster of grapes is part of one of the children's groups on the Water Avenue.
♦ 244-245-246-247

From War to Peace

187 FAUN WITH GRAPES 86
A delicate and spiritual work by Jacques Houzeau (1624-1691), relatively modern in comparison to the copy of the Queen of Sweden's Faun by Hurtrelle. This white marble term was carved between 1684 and 1687.
Height: 9'5".

THE SUPREMACY OF APOLLO

188 THE CEILING OF THE APOLLO DRAWING ROOM
189 The Apollo Drawing Room is the last room in the State Apartment, in the northern part of the central section, just before the War Drawing Room and the Hall of Mirrors. It was once the throne room.
Charles Le Brun asked a brilliant young painter, Charles de La Fosse, to paint Apollo's chariot inside an oval on the compartmented, vaulted ceiling. The sun god stands in his chariot pulled by four horses; it is morning, and he emerges from the sea, the realm of Tethys, to begin his journey around the earth. He is escorted by the four seasons: Spring, a young woman carrying a basket of flowers; below, Bacchus or Autumn, with his grapes and a cup being filled with wine; Winter, a shivering old man with a white beard warming himself over a brazier; above him we see Ceres or Summer, with her sickle and stalks of wheat.
In the lower section of the painting are two women, one representing Royal Splendour, and the other, France, wearing a cloak covered with fleurs-de-lis.
In the four corners of the ceiling La Fosse painted figures seated on globes, "denoting the four parts of the world." These can be identified by "their faces, their clothing, various symbolic elements, by figures representing the principal rivers of the earth." Surrounding the four continents, sculpted women sound trumpets "to proclaim the renown of his Majesty's glorious achievements throughout the world."
Four paintings, alternating with the continents, take their themes from ancient history, but are in fact praising the King's grandeur: "Vespasian ordering the construction of the Coliseum," "Augustus overseeing the construction of the port of Mycenae" (an allusion to the port of Cherbourg), "Porus, defeated, brought before Alexander," and "Coriolanus lifting the siege of Rome at the request of his mother Veturia."

190 THE SUN VASES 58
191 Two identical vases were carved by Drouilly and 59
192 Dugoulon between 1684 and 1688. They stand on the broad staircase overlooking Latona, at the east-west axis "Observation Point." They replace the sphinxes ridden by the children created by Sarrazin and Lerambert, transferred to the South Parterre.
Height: 6'6".

193 THE FOUNTAIN OF LATONA
Fountains playing.
♦ 111-194-195-224-225

194 LYCIAN PEASANTS
Transformed into amphibians
♦ 111-193-195-224-225

195 LATONA AND HER CHILDREN
Original marble
♦ 111-193-194-224-225

196 THE END OF THE SUN'S PATH
Sun setting beyond the Grand Canal axis

197 THE FOUNTAIN OF APOLLO → Map
Le Brun suggested making Louis XIII's Fountain of the Swans into an immense pool from which Apollo would emerge in all his splendour. This pool was situated at the end of the Green Carpet, before the perspective of the Grand Canal. The drawing he did, heavily inspired by Guido Reni's "Aurora" in the Rospigliosi Palace, and the classical group, the "Ludovisi Ares," was perfect for the style of a sculptor such as Jean-Baptiste Tubi. Tubi composed the lead group installed in 1671. It was immediately gilded. Tubi depicted the god seated as if he were straining against the force of the wind, not standing as was the classical tradition. The chariot is hitched to four spirited horses and leaves the sea to illuminate the world. Surrounding him, four tritons, alternating with sea monsters, blow on conch shells and proclaim the glory of the Sun King.
♦ 213-214-215-222-223

198 GALATEA 158
♦ 58-59

199 ACIS PLAYING THE FLUTE 156
♦ 58-59

200 INO 154
Ino, who later became Leucothea, was carved by Joseph Rayol (1655-1718) between 1685 and 1688. She was placed in the Grove of the Domes in 1690. In the 19th century, she met with the same fate as the other statues in the grove and was taken to Saint-Cloud. She holds a shell intended for "the offerings of sailors."

201 ARION 160
Jean Raon (1630-1707) carved the poet from Lesbos in white marble and engraved his signature on it: *"Joan Raon parisiensis 1695"*.
Arion is shown singing to the gods; he holds a lyre, not a zither as in the legend.
Height: about 5'2".

203 APOLLO TENDED BY THE NYMPHS → Map
After the sun brings the day to a close
It is with Tethys he seeks his repose
Like the sun, Louis, too, must rest his soul
To fulfil each day
His regal role

(La Fontaine)

The grotto of Tethys finds its antecedents in the Italian and French Renaissance nymphaea such as the famous grottoes at the Château de Saint-Germain-en-Laye where Louis XIV was born. The idea for the grotto is attributed to Charles Perrault. It was situated at the site of the lower

The Supremacy of Apollo

chapel drawing room, and given a sculpted decorative scheme of unusual magnificence, unlike anything known in antiquity.

Girardon and Regnaudin were commissioned to do the central group, portraying "Apollo tended by the nymphs." Girardon carved Apollo, the kneeling nymph drying his feet, the standing nymph pouring him water, and a third nymph on her knees holding a ewer. The three other figures are by Regnaudin. This monumental group was sculpted between 1666 and 1675; its elegance and scale constitute a high point of 17th century sculpture.

After the destruction of the grotto, the Girardon and Regnaudin groups, the Marsy and Guérin horses accompanying them and the statues of Acis and Galatea were taken to the Grove of the Domes (page 134) and then to the Marsh.

Finally, in 1774, the painter Hubert Robert devised a new theatrical setting to accommodate them: an artificial grotto with rocks and running streams, now known as the Grove of Apollo's Baths. The architect Thévenin and the sculptor Boucher carved the rocks.

Height: 8'1".

204
205 THE SUN HORSES
Sculpted by Balthazar and Gaspard Marsy between 1668 and 1675; an excellent example of the elegance and exquisite modeling so typical of the French tradition. → Map

206
207 DETAILS OF THE APOLLO GROUP
Photographs on pages 206 to 212.
♦ 202-203 → Map

213 APOLLO BY TUBI
♦ 196-197-214-215-222-223 → Map

214
215 APOLLO'S CHARIOT
in the morning light.
♦ 196-197-213-222-223 → Map

216
217 THE KING'S BEDCHAMBER
The central Drawing Room, situated at the intersection of the château and garden axes, became, in 1701, eighteen years after the Court took up residence there, the King's Bedchamber, the sanctuary of the divine-right monarchy. It was here that the Sun-King slept during the last fourteen years of his life. On August 31, 1715, after hearing the prayers for the dying recited by the Cardinal de Rohan, Louis XIV uttered his last words (taken from an account by the duke of Saint-Simon): *"Those were the last blessings of the Church." The Cardinal was the last man he spoke to. He repeated several times, "Nunc et in hora mortis", then said, "O my God, hasten to my side." Those were his last words. He was unconscious all night, and the long death-struggle ended on Sunday, September 1st, at a quarter past eight in the morning, three days before his seventy-seventh birthday, in the seventy-second year of his reign."*

After his anointing in Rheims on September 25, 1722, Louis XV returned to Versailles after seven years of absence. The bedchamber was refurnished in a rich crimson summer brocade for the occasion. The brocade hanging there today was rewoven in Lyons after the original fabric.

Like his great-grandfather, the "Well-Beloved" continued to use this noble room for the "rising" and "retiring" ceremonies, the "introductions" of newcomers to the court and the "Court-attended" dinners. But in 1738, at the age of twenty-eight, Louis XV decided to stop sleeping in this magnificent room, as it was intolerable during the severe winters, despite the two slate-blue marble fireplaces installed in 1761 to replace the violet-brecciated one from Louis XIV's day.

From 1738 onwards, Louis XV slept in the new bedchamber created by Gabriel in the private suite, but he continued to use his grandfather's bedchamber for the daily "rising" and "retiring" ceremonies.

After the death of his grandfather, Louis XVI never slept in this room, but had it furnished in 1785. He was present every morning and night for the two ceremonies.

Louis XV and Louis XVI made a point of preserving the decor installed during Louis XIV's reign. Under the cap-shaped white ceiling symbolizing the canopy of heaven, beautifully carved and gilded panelling remains as evidence of the talent of sculptors unfortunately forgotten: Pierre Taupin, Marin Belan, André le Goupil and Jean Dugoulon. The wood-panelled walls are divided into three sections and spaced by Corinthian pilasters. The central wall section consists of a glass chimneypiece and a fireplace; above the doors in the side wall sections, oval paintings are flanked by delightful carved figures holding a garland of flowers.

On either side of the room, above the cornice, three rectangular paintings are set into the attic: on the south side are "Saint Matthew," "Peter's Pence" (or the distinction between the secular and the spiritual), and "Saint Luke," all three by Valentin de Boulogne. Facing them are "Saint Mark" (by Valentin), "Agar in the Desert" (by Lanfranco, using the theme of the repudiated woman and her son helped by God. She is told that she will be mother to an entire people; perhaps this is an allusion to Anna of Austria and her son driven from Paris by the Fronde uprising), and last of all, "Saint John the Evangelist" (by Valentin).

The oval paintings above the doors pay homage to Christian bravery and to genius. There is "The Portrait of the Marquis d'Aytona" (author of a work about the Spanish struggle to drive back the Turks, enemies of Christendom), painted by Anthony Van Dyck, and, opposite, a self-portrait of this famous painter.

In the alcove, the overdoors portray New Testament characters: "Saint John the Baptist" (by Carraciolo) and "Saint Mary Magdalene" (by Domenichino).

In 1701, the alcove wall was topped with a large archway in which we see "a beautiful figure, representing France, seated on her trophies, under a luxurious tent; the ensemble is placed in the middle of a mosaic background." This description, written by Mansart, did not mention the sculptor, Nicolas Coustou. The two "figures of Fame sounding a trumpet" were done by Lespingola.

The decoration is both of a symbolic and a religious nature. We could say that it is like that of a sanctuary, and that the twelve stools are arranged for the twelve Apostles. It could also be said that the cube-shaped bed placed in the centre is like a tabernacle; in front of it one would kneel and remove one's hat; it is protected, as all shrines are, by a balustrade.

In Celebration of Water

We should remember that the French monarchy was unique. Since the baptism of Clovis by Saint Rémy in Rheims on Christmas Day, 496, the King of France was anointed with Holy Oil, which assured him of spiritual power, as is the case in an episcopal coronation. From then on, the King of France became a member of the Roman Catholic Church.

France was both a divine-right monarchy and the leading Christian nation (Oldest Daughter of the Church). When Louis XVI refused to sanction measures proclaimed by the National Assembly, not only was he complying with Pope Pius IV's condemnation of the Civil Constitution of Clergy (1791), but he was acting in accordance with his conscience and the oath taken at his coronation. A clash was inevitable. It was to lead to a confrontation destined to turn a thousand-year page in French history.

218 **DAYLIGHT** — 151
219 A work by the Italian sculptor Lazzaro Baldi which was listed in the classical sculpture reserve during the 18th century and placed on the north avenue of the Fountain of Apollo in 1795, replacing a figure of Abundance. The statue is of a young woman draped in a cloth. She stands on rays of sunlight and holds a small sun in her raised right hand.

218 **AIR** — 31
219 Here we see a chameleon close up; it is a symbolic addition to the statue. According to Pliny, "this wonderful animal lives on air only."
♦ 27-28

IN CELEBRATION OF WATER

220 **THE PYRAMID** — 204
221 The pool was dug in about 1668, in the form of a four-leaf clover. In 1683, it was given a circular form. François Girardon carved this once-gilded sculpture on the Pyramid. It was executed after drawings by Robert de Cotte, or, perhaps, Charles Le Brun. The "Comptes des Bâtiments du Roy" mention Girardon from 1671 onwards for this work executed between 1668 and 1670. The Pyramid is composed of four superimposed basins topped with a vase gushing water from "one tier to the next."
The lower bowl is held aloft by four mischievous-looking tritons. Above, triton children support the second basin with their raised arms. Dolphins and large crayfish carry the weight of the third and fourth basins. Lead. Height: 12'4".

222 **THE FOUNTAIN OF APOLLO** — Map
223 ♦ 196-213-214-215.

224 **THE FOUNTAIN OF LATONA** — 72
225 **AND THE LIZARD FOUNTAIN** — 73
♦ 111-193-194-195.

226 **DIANA'S BATHING NYMPHS** — 203
227 Situated below the Pyramid, this cascade is oriented so that it is back-lit as one approaches from the Water Avenue. As the water tumbles over the bas-relief (about 19'6" long and 6'6" high), the carved nymphs seem to come alive under the sparkling water; the effect was even more intense when the lead was gilded.
Girardon executed this masterpiece between 1668 and 1670. According to Charles Perrault, his brother Claude supplied the drawing; however, no drawing has come down to us today. Nevertheless, the theme which Girardon depicted is probably drawn from the painting by Domenichino of "The Hunt of Diana," now in the Borghese Gallery in Rome. There are definite similarities with Rubens' nymphs and the "Bathers" of Fragonard, which convey the same feeling of "joie de vivre" and pantheism. These qualities are also found in Renoir's work, and to some extent in the "Women Bathing" by Cézanne.

228 **THE ROCKWORK GROVE** — Map
OR THE BALLROOM
Work on this grove began in 1680. The steep terrain was dug out into a series of terraces, and when Louis XIV accepted the decoration models presented by the sculptors Le Gros and Massou, work began in earnest and was completed in 1683. The water came gushing out, falling from the top tier to the lowest basin. The cascades on eight levels were divided into three sections by other cascades inside straight marble ramps. The ensemble was decorated with Madagascan shells, as it is today.
In the centre of this oval grove, there was an "island," on which dancers or musicians could stand. It was paved with marble and surrounded by a "river." The spectators could sit on grass seats facing the cascades.
Changes began in 1690. The central island and its canals were removed to make room for a platform. The white marble rims of the cascades were replaced with pink Languedoc marble, and water jets replaced the gushing water.
Meanwhile, gilded-lead garden furnishings were brought in: vases by Le Comte and Le Hongre stood at the upper level, while candlestands by Mazeline, Jouvenet, Le Gros and Massou were set up in the lower area. Candalabra in rock crystal were set on these stands during festivities.
The floral decoration appeared in 1691. Three hundred carnations, one hundred double gillyflowers, two hundred and fifty veronicas and two thousand one hundred and fifty white Dame's violets were planted.

229 **THE FOUNTAIN OF SATURN** — 272
♦ 57-110.

230 **THE WATER PARTERRE: THE SEINE** — 26
The esplanade in front of the château is undoubtedly the part of the gardens which created the most problems and for which the most projects were made. It eventually became the Water Parterre we know today (between 1683 and 1685), with its two large symmetrical expanses of water. In the end the marble rims

In Celebration of Water

were not adorned with statues from the Great Commission of 1674, but with an ensemble of statues in bronze, a metal thought to be imperishable. 'The reclining statues of men represent the principal rivers of France, as those of women represent the smaller rivers'.
They are placed in alternation with nymphs and groups of children standing at the corners of the pools. The statues were cast by the Keller brothers between 1687 and 1690.
Charles Le Brun had originally designed two very large groups, dedicated to the glory of Venus and Tethys, for the centre of each pool. The project never came to fruition, but in the last century, when Louis II of Bavaria built his "imitation" Versailles at Herrenchiemsee, he had the two pyramids placed in his pools, where they create a very curious effect.
♦ 112

231 THE WATER PARTERRE: THE LOIRET 7
Thomas Regnaudin was paid for the wax models of the Loire and Loiret rivers in 1686; they were cast by the Keller brothers in 1689. The Loiret is a lovely woman reclining on the rim of the south pool, next to the Loire.

232 THE WATER PARTERRE: NYMPH 23
This nymph with the beautiful radiant face is accompanied by a child handing her a bird. The following inscriptions can be found on an oar: "*Fondv par les Kellers 1688*" and "*P. le Gros F*".

233 THE WATER PARTERRE: THE GARONNE 19
The satisfied look on the face of this bearded man may mean that a large part of this river is navigable.
Coysevox was paid for his wax models of the Garonne and Dordogne rivers in 1686. An inscription on an urn reads: "*Fondv par les Kellers Svisses 1688.*"

234 THE WATER PARTERRE: NYMPH 22
This nymph holding a garland leans nonchalantly on a dolphin; a triton is at her side. She adorns the North Pool. There are two inscriptions on the plaque: "*Fondu par les Kellers 1688*" and "*P. le Gros F.*" Le Gros made his wax model in 1670; it was quite a while before the bronze was made.

235 THE WATER PARTERRE: THE LOIRE 8
The use of reclining human figures to represent rivers dates back to antiquity. The most famous examples are two statues of the Tiber and the Nile (dating from the 2nd century A.D., but inspired by even more ancient models from the Hellenistic period) which Pope Julius II bought in 1513 and placed in the Belvedere Courtyard in the Vatican. François I had a copy in bronze of the Tiber made for Fontainebleau but it was destroyed in 1792.
Louis XIV commissioned Pierre Bourdy to do another replica for the Marly gardens in 1688. This marble statue is now in the Tuileries gardens.
After the Treaty of Tolentino in 1797, Bonaparte had a number of famous classical works, including the Nile, taken from Rome to Paris; they were, however, returned in 1815. Though the Nile was returned to the Vatican, the classical Tiber remained in the Louvre.

The Loire by Thomas Regnaudin was wholly inspired by the Tiber. It bears the inscriptions: "*Fondv par les Kellers 1689*" and "*Tho Regnaudin 1689.*"
We know that Regnaudin was paid in 1686 for his wax models of the Loire and the Loiret.

236 THE WATER PARTERRE: THE MARNE 25
Étienne Le Hongre was paid for his wax models of the Marne, the Seine and several nymphs in 1687.
The river is personified by a woman holding a cornucopia, symbol of abundance in the regions she crosses. She rests against an oar held by a cupid carrying a garland.
The bronze bears the inscriptions: "*Fondv par les Kellers 1689*", "*Le Hongre F.*"

237 THE WATER PARTERRE: THE SAONE 14
Tubi portrayed this river as a naked woman leaning on an urn and holding spikes of wheat. Nearby, a cupid holds a garland of wheat and grapes.
Tubi was paid for the wax models of the Saône and Rhône rivers in 1687, and they were cast in the same year by the Kellers. An inscription on the neck of the urn reads: "*Baptiste Tuby F. Fondv par les Kellers.*"

238 THE WATER PARTERRE: NYMPH 10
Étienne Le Hongre chose to depict this nymph in the company of a crowned "zephyr" with butterfly wings. The clay model was executed between 1684 and 1686. The bronze bears the inscription: "*Fondv par les Kellers 1690.*"

239 THE WATER PARTERRE: THE RHONE 13
Tubi was paid for the wax models of the Rhône and Saône rivers in 1687. The impetuous god leans on an oar and lies next to a cupid. On the oar we read: "*Baptiste Tuby fondv par les Kellers.*"

THE THEME OF CHILDHOOD

240 FOUNTAIN IN THE "LOWER GARDEN" OF THE GRAND TRIANON
The pool is adorned with a child playing amid clusters of grapes. It is probably one of the figures from the Fountain of Bacchus (or Autumn) by Balthazar and Gaspard Marsy, which was taken to the Trianon.

241 VASE DEPICTING MARS' CHILDHOOD 70
♦ 72

242 CANDLESTAND IN THE ROCKWORK GROVE (DETAIL) → Map
♦ 228

The Theme of Childhood

243 FIGURES ON VASES IN THE TRIANON
One of the most remarkable views at Versailles, and perhaps one of the lesser known, can be seen from the Fountain of the Maidens. This pool, adorned with four young girls in lead, is situated above the Hall of Classical Sculptures. This point overlooks the Hall of Chestnut Trees and its flower parterres, and the avenue in the lower parterre at the Grand Trianon; the eye then travels to the end of the Grand Canal, with its water glistening in the sun.
Two large once-gilded lead vases by Robert Le Lorrain (1666-1743) border the Fountain of the Maidens. The covers of the vases are carved with delightful figures of children, adding an original touch.

244 THE WATER AVENUE 188
245 OR AVENUE OF THE MARMOSETS to
246 To the north, this is the axis running from the 202
247 Pyramid and the Bathing Nymphs to the Fountain of the Dragon and the Fountain of Neptune. The Perrault brothers took credit for the idea for this decoration. Le Brun probably furnished the drawings of the seven groups of children: girls and boys placed in pairs.
On each little fountain we find three bronze children standing on a pedestal in white marble with icicle motifs. They hold a pink marble bowl from which water gushes and cascades over the figures.
In 1678 the original ensemble of fourteen groups was enlarged with eight other groups, intended for the half-moon of the Dragon Fountain.
An important change took place in 1688 when the King ordered that all the lead figures be recast in bronze and that the floral decoration on the basins be removed.
These figures who play, dance, sing and make music form a delightful picture. Moving from the top of the walk downwards, we find three tritons by Le Gros, three dancers by Le Gros, two cupids and a little girl by Le Hongre, three children around a tree trunk by Lerambert, and three musicians by Lerambert. There are also three satyrs by Le Gros, three terms by Lerambert, two girls and a boy playing with fish by Mazeline, three hunters by Mazeline, three children by Buirette and three little girls by Buirette.

248 BRONZE VASE IN THE SOUTH PARTERRE →
249 ♦ 22-23-71-76-77-128-129-162 Map

248 THE CHILDREN'S ISLAND
249 This fountain, hidden between the Green Ring 177
and the Star Grove, is brought to life by a delightful group of six children sitting on an island, while two others swim and play in the water. The ensemble was carved by Jean Hardy (1653-1737), and in 1710 it was placed in its present spot. While several historians believe it to be the decorative scheme from a pool at the Porcelain Trianon, other more recent authorities have said that it is from a pool in the former Water Theatre, located on the present site of the Green Ring.

250 THE WATER PARTERRE: NYMPH 22
The two nymphs by Pierre Le Gros are on the south rim of the North Pool. In 1670 the sculptor received an initial payment for his model. Additional information is provided by the inscriptions: "*Fondv par les Kellers 1688*" and "*P. Le Gros F.*".
The nymph is crowned with reed leaves. She leans on a dolphin and looks towards him. In her raised right hand she carries a garland of reeds held by a young triton at the other end.
♦ 116-121-122-123

251 THE WATER PARTERRE: 23
NYMPH WITH CHILD (DETAIL)
This is the second nymph by Le Gros in the Water Parterre. Here we see a close-up of the child holding out a bird to her; meanwhile she has turned and leans on an oar and the prow. The sculptor was paid for his model in 1685. On the oar is inscribed: «*Fondv par les Kellers 1688*» and «*P Le Gros F.*».
♦ 116-121-122-123

252 THE WATER PARTERRE: 30
GROUP OF CHILDREN
Corneille Van Clève was paid 2,250 livres in 1687 for the wax models of this group of children and fighting animals. A crowned cupid holds a reed, another blows into a shell and a third carries a quiver. The group was cast by Aubry and Roger in 1690.
♦ 116-121-122-123

253 THE WATER PARTERRE: 18
CHILD WITH A MIRROR
There are eight groups of children on the Water Parterre. Each reclining nymph or river is accompanied by a child.
On pages 250 and 251 the bronzes are shown in the cold blue morning light, while on pages 252 and 253 we see them in the warm twilight, when their patina takes on a golden tone.
♦ 116-121-122-123

254 TRITON FROM THE CASCADE
The Cascade in the Grand Trianon gardens was built by Jules Hardouin-Mansart in 1701. The five-level fountain is in pink and white marble, and is adorned with gilded-lead figures. We see a man and a woman seated on volutes at the top, tritons carrying two marble bowls, symmetrically placed lions, bas-reliefs, etc.

254 THE WATER PARTERRE: 13
255 GROUP OF CHILDREN (DETAIL)
This group by Simon Mazière is on the southwest corner of the South Pool. The sculptor was paid in 1683 for his model.
Aubry, Bonvallet, Roger and Taupin were paid for the bronze cast in 1690.
♦ 116-121-122-123

255 FOUNTAIN OF CERES 172
♦ 70

256 NIGHT ON THE WATER PARTERRE 18
♦ 122-230-253

LIST OF ARTISTS CITED

*Figures in roman type indicate
pages on which illustrations appear.
Figures in italic type indicate
citations in the notes, the references
being to the page numbers on the left of the text.*

AGESANDER (Ist century B.C.),
sculptor
101

ANDRÉ Antoine (?-1710),
sculptor
160

ANGUIER Michel (1612-1686),
sculptor
134

ARCIS Marc (1655-1739),
sculptor
62

ATHENODORUS (Ist century B.C.),
sculptor
101

AUBRY François (known from 1679 to 1690),
sculptor and metal-founder
122, 252, 254, 255

BABEL Jean-Baptiste (18th century),
sculptor
166, 167

BALDI Lazzaro (1624-1703)
sculptor
218, 219

BALLIN Claude (1615-1678),
goldsmith
22, 23, 76, 77, 128, 129, *82*

BAROIS François (1656-1726),
sculptor
148

BELAN Marin (late 17th - early 18th century),
sculptor
216, 217

BERNINI Gian Lorenzo (1598-1680),
sculptor, architect
28, *100, 107*

BERTIN Claude (?-1705),
sculptor
79

BOLOGNE Jean de (1529-1608),
sculptor
86, 87

BONVALLET (known from 1686 to 1691),
sculptor and metal founder
254, 255

BOUCHARDON Edmé (1698-1762),
sculptor
106

BOUCHER François (1703-1770),
painter
85

BOUCHER Yves-Eloi (1738-1782),
sculptor
202, 203

BOURDY Pierre (17th-18th century),
sculptor
235

BUIRETTE Jacques (1631-1699),
sculptor
121, 155, *86, 87, 244, 245, 246, 247*

BUYSTER Philippe (1595-1698),
sculptor
53, 182, 183

CAFFIERI Philippe (1634-1716),
sculptor
58, 59

CARLIER Martin (?-1700?),
sculptor
147

CARRACIOLO Giovanni Battista
(1570-1637), painter
216, 217

CLEOMENES (Ist century B.C.),
sculptor
147, 166, 167

CLÉRION Jean-Jacques (1637-1714),
sculptor
140, 148, *147, 166, 167*

CORNU Jean (1650-1710),
sculptor
47, *72*

COTELLE Jean (1642-1708),
painter
92

COTTE Robert de (1656-1735),
architect
24, 25, 92, 220, 221

COUSTOU Nicolas (1658-1733),
sculptor
216, 217

*****COYSEVOX** Antoine (1640-1720),
sculptor
20, 21, 145, 168, 233, *117, 138, 146, 147, 166, 167*

DARDIGNAC (18th century),
painter and decorator
108

DEDIEU Jean (1646-1727),
sculptor
156, 178, 94

DESCHAMPS Joseph (1743-1788),
sculptor
106

DESJARDINS Martin (1637-1694),
sculptor
38, 39, 152, *86, 87, 118, 119*

DOIDALCES (3rd century B.C.),
sculptor
145

DOMENICHINO (Domenico Zampieri),
(1581-1641), painter
216, 217, 226, 227

* also COYZEVOX

DOSSIER Nicolas (known from 1664 to 1701), sculptor
29

DROUILLY Jean (?-1698),
sculptor
52, 190, 191, 192

DUFOUR Alexandre (1760-1835),
architect
56

DUGOULON Jean (?-1687),
sculptor
85, *173, 190, 191, 192, 216, 217*

EPIGONOS (3rd century B.C.)
sculptor
161

FLAMEN Anselme (1647-1717),
sculptor
154, *27, 86, 87, 134, 166, 167*

FOGGINI Giovanni Battista
(1652-1725), sculptor
117

FOLIOT Toussaint (18th century),
sculptor
166, 167

FRAGONARD Jean-Honoré
(1732-1806), painter
226, 227

FRÉMERY Nicolas (?-after 1687),
sculptor
147

FRÉMIN René (1672-1744),
sculptor
134

GABRIEL Ange-Jacques (1698-1782),
architect
81, 85, *217*

GABRIEL Jacques (1667-1742),
architect
85

GIRARDON François (1628-1715),
sculptor
42, 43, 109, 110, 115, 202, 203, 207,
209, 212, 220, 221, 226, 227, 229,
*27, 57, 58, 59, 62, 79, 102, 103, 131,
135, 139, 154, 166, 167, 170, 181*

GONDOUIN Jacques (1737-1818),
architect, decorator, and designer
166, 167

GOUJON Jean (1515-1567?)
sculptor and architect
43

GOY Jean-Baptiste (1666-1738),
sculptor
18

GRANIER Pierre (1635-1715),
sculptor
52, 103, 157, *94*

GRÉGOIRE René (19th century),
sculptor
19

GUÉRIN Gilles (1609-1678),
sculptor
27, 49, 58, 59, 203

GUIDI Domenico (1625-1701),
sculptor
55, 59, 182, 183

HARDY Jean (1635-1737),
sculptor
241, 248, 249, 254, *72, 78*

HÉRARD Gérard-Léonard (1637?-1675),
sculptor
52

HOUZEAU Jacques (1624-1691),
sculptor
51, 118, 119, 187

HULOT Guillaume (1660?-1724),
sculptor
79

HURTRELLE Simon (1648-1724),
sculptor
58, 149, 156, *72, 94, 187*

HUTINOT Pierre (1616-1679),
sculptor
40, 41, *79*

JOUVENET Noël (?-1716),
sculptor
51, 146, *228*

KELLER Jean-Balthazar (1638-1702),
metal-founder
86, 87, *112, 113, 117, 118, 119, 144, 145,
230, 231, 232, 233, 234, 235, 236,
237, 238, 239, 250, 251*

KELLER Jean-Jacques (1635-1700),
metal-founder
86, 87, *112, 113, 117, 118, 119, 144, 145,
230, 231, 232, 233, 234, 235, 236,
237, 238, 239, 250, 251*

*****LA FOSSE** Charles de (1636-1716),
painter
188, 189

LANFRANCO Giovanni (1582-1647),
painter
216, 217

LA PERDRIX Michel de (1641?-1681),
sculptor
50

LAVIRON Pierre (1650-1685?),
sculptor
63, 114, 115, 116, 123, *72*

*****LE BRUN** Charles (1619-1690),
painter
*26, 27, 28, 29, 30, 31, 32,
33, 34, 35, 36, 37, 38, 39, 40, 41,
42, 43, 44, 45, 46, 50, 51,
52, 53, 57, 70, 95, 110, 136, 137, 156,
166, 167, 168, 171, 172, 188, 189,
197, 220, 221, 230, 244, 245, 246, 247*

* also LAFOSSE
* also LEBRUN

LE COMTE Louis (1650-1681), sculptor
171, 72, 86, 87, 166, 167, 228

LEFÈVRE Armand (17th century), sculptor
152

LE GOUPIL André (?1662-?1715), sculptor
85, 216, 217

***LE GROS** Pierre (1629-1714), sculptor
30, 32, 54, 107, 116, 123, 125, 131, 143, 186, 232, 234, 245, 246, 247, 250, 251, 86, 87, 134, 166, 167, 228, 244

LE HONGRE Étienne (1628-1690), sculptor
17, 28, 107, 112, 124, 130, 172, 218, 219, 230, 236, 238, 244, 228, 245, 246, 247

LE LORRAIN Robert (1666-1743), sculptor
243

***LEMOYNE** François (1688-1737), painter
136, 137

LE NOTRE André (1613-1700), architect, garden-designer and decorator
27, 71, 80, 86, 87, 100, 111, 126, 127

LEOCHARES (4th century B.C.) sculptor
38, 39, 139

LERAMBERT Louis (1620-1670), sculptor
244, 245, 190, 191, 192, 246, 247

LESPAGNANDELLE Mathieu (1616-1689), sculptor
50, 159, 160, 94

* also LE CONTE
* also LEGROS
* also LEMOINE

LESPINGOLA François (1644-1705), sculptor
100, 121, 161, 216, 217

LE VAU Louis (1612-1670), architect
24, 25, 27, 79, 84, 86, 87, 88, 89, 166, 167

LYSIPPUS (4th century B.C.), sculptor
38, 39, 61

MAGNIER Laurent (about 1619-1700), sculptor
158

MAGNIER Philippe (1647-1715), sculptor
44, 45, 113, 135, 159, 94, 134

MANSART (Jules Hardouin-Mansart) (1646-1708), architect
126, 127, 24, 25, 27, 72, 73, 78, 79, 86, 87, 90, 92, 111, 134, 166, 167, 216, 217, 241, 254

MARSY Balthazar (1628-1674), sculptor
95, 111, 179, 193, 194, 195, 204, 205, 224, 225, 27, 57, 58, 59, 86, 87, 163, 164, 165, 203, 240

MARSY Gaspard (1629-1681), sculptor
36, 37, 95, 104, 105, 111, 133, 179, 193, 195, 204, 205, 224, 225, 240, 57, 58, 59, 86, 87, 118, 119, 163, 164, 165, 203

MASSOU Benoît (1627-1684), sculptor
31, 33, 166, 167, 228

MAZELINE Pierre (1632-1708), sculptor
46, 139, 228, 244, 245, 246, 247

MAZIÈRE Simon (1649-1720), sculptor
62, 170, 180, 181, 186, 254, 255

MÉLO Barthélémy de
(late 17th century to early 18th century),
sculptor
157, *94*

MICHELANGELO Buonarotti
(1475-1564), painter, sculptor and
architect
101

MIGNARD Pierre (1612-1695),
painter
140, 143, 156, 157, 159

MIQUE Richard (1728-1794),
architect
64, 65, 106, 66, *67, 108*

*****MOSNIER** Michel (known
from 1671 to 1686), sculptor
147, 161

NATOIRE Charles-Joseph (1700-1777),
painter
85

NOEL Edmé Antony Paul
(known as Tony NOEL)
(1848-1909), sculptor
163, 164, 165

PERRAULT Charles (1628-1688),
writer
203, 226, 227, 244, 245, 246, 247

PERRAULT Claude (1613-1688),
architect
226, 227, 244, 245, 246, 247

PHIDIAS (5th century B.C.),
sculptor, painter and goldsmith
145, 169

POLYDORUS (Ist century B.C.)
sculptor
101

POULLETIER Jean (1653-1719),
sculptor
78, 79, 122, 153, 253

* also MONNIER

POUSSIN Nicolas (1594-1665),
painter
176, 177, *55, 74, 107, 110, 182, 183, 185*

PRAXITELES (4th century B.C.),
sculptor
54, 58, 147

PRIMATICE (Le Primaticcio) Francesco
(1504-1570), painter, sculptor and architect
18

PROU Jacques (1655-1706), sculptor
72, 78

PUGET Pierre (1620-1694), sculptor
101, 161

RAON Jean (1630-1707), sculptor
34, 35, 132, 173, 201,
86, 87, 118, 119, 134

RAYOL Joseph (1655-1718),
sculptor
158, 200, *94, 134*

REGNAUDIN Thomas (1622-1706),
sculptor
42, 70, 184, 202, 203, 206, 210,
211, 231, 235, 255,
27, 57, 58, 59, 79, 86, 87

RENI Guido (1575-1642)
painter
197

RENOIR Auguste (1841-1919),
painter
145, 226, 227

RIPA Cesare, theorist
26, 31, 33, 37, 42, 43, 50, 51, 52

ROMAIN Jules (Giulio Pippi
de Giannuzzi) (1482-1546),
painter and architect
104, 105

ROBERT Hubert (1733-1808),
painter and decorator
64, 65, 203

ROGER Léonard (known from 1663 to 1694), sculptor
26, 48, 122, 252, 254, 255

RUBENS Peter Paul (1577-1640), painter
145, 226, 227

SARRAZIN Jacques (1592-1660), sculptor
107, *190, 191, 192*

SÈVE Gilbert de (?-1698), painter
85

SIBRAYQUE Georges (?-1694), sculptor
47

SLODTZ Sébastien (1665-1726), sculptor
102

SUCHETET Auguste (1854-1932), sculptor
138

TAUPIN Pierre (1622-1734), sculptor
216, 217, 254, 255

THÉODON Jean-Baptiste (1646-1713), sculptor
74, *55, 79, 131*

THÉVENIN (18th century), architect
203

TOLÈDE (18th century), painter and decorator
108

TROY Jean-François de (1679-1752), painter
85

*****TUBI** Jean-Baptiste (1635-1700), sculptor
53, 57, 58, 59, 101, 120, 169, 196, 197, 198, 199, 213, 222, 237, 239, *79, 203*

VALENTIN DE BOULOGNE (1591-1632), painter
216, 217

VAN CLÈVE Corneille (1645-1735), sculptor
18, 132, 142, 252, *102, 118, 119*

VAN DYCK Sir Anthony (1599-1641), painter
216, 217

VERBERCKT Jacques (1704-1771), sculptor
85

VERONESE (Paolo Caliari) (1528-1588), painter
136, 137

VIGIER Philibert (1636-1719) sculptor
155

VINCI Leonardo de (1452-1519) painter, sculptor and architect
95

* also TUBY

BIBLIOGRAPHY

Sources for the Preface

— LOUIS XIV, *Manière de montrer les jardins de Versailles.*
Commentary by Simone Hoog.
Paris, 1982 - Editions de la Réunion des Musées Nationaux.
— EMANUELA KRETZULESCO-QUARANTA, *Les jardins du songe.*
Rome, 1976.

Sources for the introduction
and the texts accompanying the photographs

*The figures in italics
refer to the pages on which the texts are quoted*

— ALAIN (Emile-Auguste CHARTIER), *Préliminaires à la Mythologie.*
Paris: Ed. Paul Hartmann, 1951. — *15, 16, 173, 175, 232.*
— BACHELARD, Gaston, *La Poétique de la Rêverie.*
Paris: P.U.F., 1960. — *36, 123, 202.*
— CHANDERNAGOR, Françoise, *L'Allée du Roi.*
Paris: Julliard, 1981. — *72.*
— CHOMPRÉ and A.L. MILIN, *Dictionnaire de la Fable.*
Paris: Desray, 1801. — *31, 45, 62, 111, 116, 139, 141, 142, 159, 171, 172.*
— FRANCASTEL, Pierre, *La Sculpture de Versailles.*
Paris: Morancé, 1930. — *27, 51, 81, 131, 174.*
— GUÉRIN, Maurice de, *Poèmes.*
Paris: Société Les Belles Lettres, 1947. — *179, 186.*
— HÖLDERLIN, *Hypérion.*
Paris: Gallimard, 1973. — *172, 173, 174, 175.*
— LA FONTAINE, Jean de, *Les Amours de Psyché et de Cupidon.*
Paris: Biliotheca Magna, 1939. — *198, 199, 202, 209, 210.*
— LOUIS XIV, cited in *Versailles le Palais du Soleil* by Edouard Guillou.
Paris: Ed. d'Art et d'Histoire, 1963. — *173, 189.*
— MARIE, Alfred, *Naissance de Versailles.*
Paris: Vincent Fréal et Cie, 1968. — *137, 251.*
— MARIE, Alfred, *Mansart à Versailles.*
Paris: Ed. Jacques Fréal, 1972. — *241.*
— MARIE, Alfred, *Versailles au Temps de Louis XIV.*
Paris: Imprimerie Nationale, 1976. — *128, 217.*
— MAURICHEAU-BEAUPRE, Charles, *Versailles.*
Paris: Draeger et Verve, 1949. — *153, 168.*
— MICHELET, Jules, *Histoire de France.*
Paris: J. Hetzel et Cie, XIXe siècle. — *163.*
— NIETZSCHE, Frédéric, *La Naissance de la Tragédie.*
Paris: Denoël-Gonthier, 1964. — *179.*
— NOLHAC, Pierre de, *Les Jardins de Versailles.*
Asnières: Manzi-Joyant et Cie, 1905. — *36, 43, 48, 98, 116, 128, 156, 159, 202, 249, 251.*
— NOLHAC, Pierre de, *La Création de Versailles.*
Versailles: Lib. Bernard, 1901. — *80, 95, 146, 161, 166, 241.*
— OVIDE, *Les Métamorphoses.*
Paris: Flammarion - G.F., 1966. — *29, 59, 62, 171, 194, 195, 199, 227, 254.*
— PINATEL, Christiane, *Les Statues Antiques des Jardins de Versailles.*
Paris: Ed. A. et J. Picard et Cie, 1963. — *60.*
— RIPA Cesare, *Inconologia* (1644). — *27, 51.*
— SAINT-SIMON (Louis de Rouvroy, Duc de), *Mémoires.* — *62, 71.*

- VAN der KEMP, Gérald and LEMOINE, Pierre, *Versailles et Trianon*.
  Versailles: Ed. d'Art Lys, 1979. — *86, 137, 166, 189, 217.*
- VALÉRY, Paul, *L'Ame et la Danse*.
  Paris: Gallimard, 1944. — *179.*
- VERLET, Pierre, *Versailles*.
  Paris: Lib. Arthème Fayard, 1961. — *71, 104, 128, 137, 173, 217, 221.*
- VIRGILE, *Géorgiques*.
  Paris: Flammarion - G.F., 1967. — *59, 74, 90, 174, 175, 186.*
- VOLTAIRE (François Marie AROUET), *Le Siècle de Louis XIV*.
  Paris: Library of Elie Roy, 1828-1912. — *15, 16.*

The passages in the text between quotation marks were sometimes taken from old guides; historians specializing in Versailles, like Pierre de Nolhac and Alfred Marie, often quoted these guides without citing the author.

Old Sources for Study of the Versailles Sculpture

Archives Nationales : "La Maison du Roy"

- "*Comptabilité Générale - Comptes des Bâtiments du Roy*" - O^1 2129 to 2216; from 1668 to 1716, published by Jules Guiffrey (1881: Paris, Imprimerie Nationale).
- *General inventory of sculpture, 1692-1695* ($O^1 1977^A$ and $O^1 1977^B$).
- *Condition of the sculpture, 1694-1790.*
  17th-18th century inventory (O^1 1967).
- *General inventory, 1707* (O^1 1976^A and 1976^B).
- *Inventory: early 18th century,* (O^1 1968).
- *General inventory, 1722* (O^1 1969^A and 1969^B).
- *Report from the Provisional Committee on Fine Arts, 1791-1795* (F^{17} 1270).

17th and 18th Century Sources

- MADEMOISELLE de SCUDÉRY: *La Promenade de Versailles*, 1669.
- JEAN DE LA FONTAINE: *Les Amours de Psyché et de Cupidon*, 1669.
- ANDRÉ FÉLIBIEN: *Description sommaire du chasteau de Versailles*, 1674; *Description du chasteau de Versailles*, 1685 (several editions).
- COMBES: *Explication historique de ce qu'il y a de plus remarquable dans la Maison royale de Versailles et en celle de Monsieur à Saint-Cloud*, 1681.
- DE LA GASTINE: *Description du château de Versailles...*, 1687.
- LOUIS XIV: *Manière de montrer les Jardins de Versailles*, 1689-1705 edition.
- THOMASSIN: *Recueil des figures, groupes, termes, fontaines, vases et autres ornements tels qu'ils se voyent à présent dans le château et parc de Versailles*, 1694.
- DAME JOURDAIN: *Remarques historiques sur les figures, termes et vases qui ornent les jardins du Parc de Versailles...*, January 1695.
- PIGANIOL de LA FORCE: *Nouvelles descriptions des chasteaux et parc de Versailles et de Marly*, 1701 (several editions).
- MONICART: *Versailles immortalisé*, 1720.
- DEZALLIER d'ARGENVILLE: *Vie des fameux sculpteurs...*, 1740.
- DEZALLIER d'ARGENVILLE: *Voyage pittoresque des Environs de Paris, ou description des Maisons royales, châteaux et autres lieux de plaisance...*, 1755 (several editions).

PRINTED BY
IMPRIMERIE DU PAROI
RECLOSES

ILLUSTRATIONS PHOTOENGRAVED
BY PHOTOGRAVURE PERENCHIO
PARIS

PHOTOENGRAVING
ON PAGES 33-85-182-202-203-216-217-228
BY BUSSIERE ARTS GRAPHIQUES
PARIS

BOUND BY S.I.R.C.
MARIGNY-LE-CHATEL

Dépôt légal 3ème trimestre 1985 — Editions d'Art Lys - 2 bis, Passage Toulouse - 78000 Versailles — Printed in France